EMPIRE R(

To Les.
Merry Christmas 2016.
Mair. x.

ALAN WHELAN

Published by

INKSTAND PRESS

EMPIRE ROAD

An Inkstand Press book
First published in Great Britain in 2015
Copyright © Alan Whelan 2015
All rights reserved.

INKSTAND PRESS
Lytham St Annes, UK
www.abhaha.com

Cover design by Deeper Blue www.wearedeeper.blue
ISBN: 978-0-9572248-1-0

For Olive, with love

CONTENTS

Map

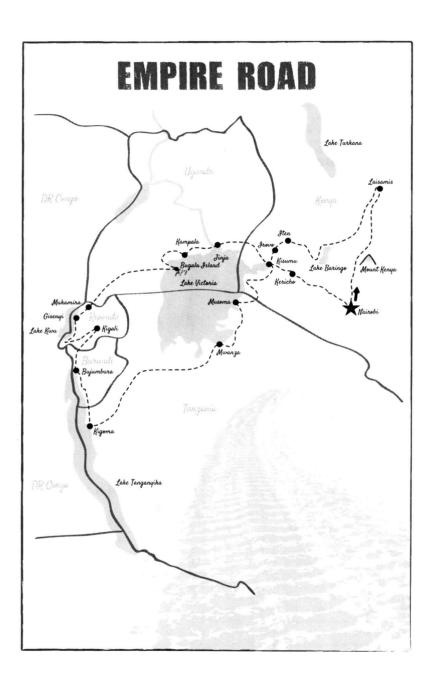

1

A KIND OF SEEING

In the half-light of the grey afternoon I peer at the framed photograph on the wall. A middle-aged woman stares into the camera lens, smiling but reserved. Her sharp face, pale and waxy, is protected from the sun by a floppy, wide-brimmed hat. The photo, taken in this house almost a hundred years ago when the sight of a white woman was enough to create gossip among the Kikuyu, hangs on the wall of the farmhouse where she once lived. For seventeen years she tried to grow coffee on 600 acres of unsuitably acid soil, but the farm on the Central Highlands was too high with too little rain to sustain the delicate plants. The venture was a failure, but her stay here, thousands of kilometres from her native Denmark, should be considered a success.

Ten kilometres from Nairobi (a dorp of only 20,000 souls on Karen Blixen's arrival in 1914), the farm once bordered the Maasai lands, and it was this potential that fired her imagination more than coffee and oxen and the details of agriculture, and led to her memoir *Out of Africa*, a homage to her beloved Kenya.

I sneak a look into the cosy library where Blixen – more used to a privileged, bourgeois lifestyle – must have spent many happy hours. Her writing recalls her time in Africa as one long journey, or safari: a new word in the English vocabulary, but familiar to her as someone who quickly learned Swahili.

I step out onto the verandah of the single-storey farmhouse. It is June. The big rains have gone, leaving the gardens lush and green. Hulks of rusting antique machinery, remnants of the original farm, are scattered throughout the plot trying to look ornamental. Rather than spectacular views of the Ngong Hills that she describes in her book, I am hemmed in by the tall hedges of a new boundary. Blixen's land has been sold off for development, and the Maasai have long been pushed west by the growth of the city.

Curtains of cloud draw across the sky and it is trying to rain, so I get on my bike and head back down Ngong Road through the district named in Blixen's honour: Karen, an upmarket neighbourhood that is now home to the Karen Country Club, Karen Coffee Garden and Karen petrol station. On my way into Nairobi, I spot Henry, the boda-boda (moto taxi rider) who yesterday helped me buy the bike in the south of the city. He waves me down on a busy corner.

He sits side-saddle on his bike, lazy boda-boda style, as he waits for a fare with half a dozen other riders. He is bundled up with a leather bomber jacket, gloves and a woolly scarf that he wraps around his head inside his helmet. I am wearing only a shirt and cargo pants and feel a sweat coming on.

'I could hear you coming,' he says, excited. 'The bike is most powerful. A sports model, I think.'

'Hardly,' I say.

My new Chinese moto is a Shineray XY175GY Sport. The most important information here is '175', because that's the capacity of the single-cylinder engine – about half the size of an average sit-on lawn mower, but with none of the comfort.

'Did I choose well for you, *mzungu*?' he asks.

'It's perfect, Henry.'

'Does the radio still produce music?' he asks.

He bends down and switches on the radio that is bolted to the left leg protector. A stream of Kenyan rap booms out.

'It is a sports bike *and* a music machine!' he says.

'Can you get the BBC?' I ask.

'Your BBC will not tell you what you need to know in Africa, *mzungu*.'

'Perhaps you're right.'

'Do you go to the Lake Victoria today?' he asks.

'In a few days. First I head north.'

He leans heavily on my pillion seat, enough to almost tip me over.

'I would not advise you go to the northern desert. I would not go. I would not take my chance with the *morani*.'

He sees my questioning look.

'The Samburu warriors. Even Kenyans cannot deal with them.'

'I'll be fine,' I say. 'The *mzungu* can look after himself.'

He casts a doubtful look then steps back and spreads his arms, which pulls his belly out of his shirt.

'One day you must return to Nairobi with this moto,' he says. 'Because I would like for myself a sports bike!'

'Henry, believe me, it's no sports bike.'

He doesn't listen. He readjusts the scarf inside his helmet.

'Where's the new helmet I gave you?' I ask.

'It is too marvellous. I will keep it for uncommon occasions.'

He slips off his seat and caresses my bike's matt green paintwork, which looks as if it's camouflaged for jungle warfare.

'But it looks like you are in the army,' he laughs. 'Maybe your army bike will frighten the *morani*!'

A woman scuffs up and calls out a destination, to which Henry is the first to answer. He swings his leg over his bike and quickly kicks the starter into life. She joins him on pillion, smacks him on the shoulder and points ahead.

'I hope to see you once more, *mzungu*,' he shouts, before pushing off into the middle of the street, bringing two lanes of traffic to a halt.

I click into first, and slip into a gap between a truck full of cattle and a fast food delivery trike.

My new bike has a tiny petrol tank and it might be difficult to get fuel in sparsely populated northern Kenya, so I consider ways carrying an extra supply. The best I can do is buy a five-litre tin can that is more often used to carry cooking oil, then some helpful guys at a petrol station lash it to a pillion footrest with thick strips of rubber cut from an old inner tube. I'm more likely to lose a wheel before that falls off.

The low cloud clears and the heat of the sun comes on, as if by a switch. I make my way to the deserted railway museum, a collection of artefacts from the golden age of Kenya Railways. Steam engines and Pullman carriages, some built in Manchester, rust in a siding. All except one. I haul myself up onto the footplate of the engine featured in the movie *Out of Africa*. Still sporting its aubergine and green livery, it has been left in fine condition by the movie producers.

Inside the museum, two staff at the entrance eat food from tin foil packages and take a few pennies from me. Glass-cased exhibits tell the story of the construction of the 'Lunatic Line', the railway from Mombasa on the Indian Ocean to Kisumu on Lake Victoria 1,000 kilometres away. Begun in 1896 in what was then the East Africa Protectorate, the mammoth logistical project took five years in what many people believed was impenetrable country. The bedevilled construction was hampered by freakish storms, searing heat, labour strikes, poor supply lines, attacks from local tribes, disease and the not-inconsiderable difficulty of building from sea level to 1,800 metres. Four workers (mostly imported Indian labourers) were killed for every mile of track laid. Lunatics? Just British colonialists doing what was expected of them.

This was the kind of undertaking that strengthened Britain's colonial ambitions in Africa and ensured those territories remained pink on the map: the traditional cartographical colour of the British Empire. Nothing was

13

going to stop the tide of progress, the British 'you're-either-with-us-or-you're-against-us' kind. The old ticket machines, steel badges and signs, and sepia photographs lining the walls of the museum simultaneously speak of the past and signal a tentative dream of the future, still kept alive, when this part of Africa will be crisscrossed by railway tracks. Perhaps it is no more than a dream: the line to Lake Victoria has fallen into chronic disrepair and is currently out of action.

I look forward to heading in the direction of the railway line, but for now I ride off into the sea of three million people sweating under an empty sky. Nairobi, once an insignificant outpost before the railway made it the most populous city in East Africa, is a stew of tribes. To my eyes it seems that no two people have anything in common. Some have almost black skin, pointy, shaven heads and darkened whites of the eyes, big hands and soft voices; some are round-faced and wide-nosed with large heads and high foreheads; others are slightly built with deep lines in their faces and sleepy expressions; some women have sharp, well-defined features and taut skin with epicanthic folds above beautiful eyes. I don't yet know the names of the tribes, but I hope to fill in some gaps on my journey around Lake Victoria, the reason I am here.

A little smaller than Ireland, Lake Victoria is Africa's biggest lake and its shoreline is shared between three countries: Kenya, Uganda and Tanzania. My plan is to ride around its perimeter as far as I can, and also take in Rwanda and Burundi, two small, mountainous countries west of the lake. As one of the defining geographical features of East Africa, the lake acts like gravity, drawing people to fish in its waters, travel between shoreline ports and live along its tributaries, which include the White Nile.

The lake was also the focus for that spearhead of British colonialism: the Great Victorian Explorer. The most celebrated – Dr David Livingstone, Sir Henry Morton Stanley, Sir Richard Burton and John Hanning Speke – did not seek riches by exploiting natural resources, or trafficking in human misery like the slave traders. They explored, largely, for the sake of exploring; to see where it would take them, in Africa, and in life. Even Stanley, an ambitious and hardbitten journalist who arrived in Africa looking for a story, underwent months of harsh trekking before he found Livingstone. Stanley then confirmed the source of the Nile by circumnavigating Lake Victoria, and later became the first European to trace the entire course of the River Congo to the Atlantic, a mind-boggling feat of endurance. His detractors, of which there are many, cannot say he wasn't born with the explorer's gene.

There are many key sites of Victorian exploration that I am sure to discover as I weave my way around the lake, which I hope will provide a little inspiration for my own journey.

Of course, where explorers trod, commerce was never far behind. Much of "Darkest Africa" – so named because early cartographers left the unexplored interior black – would soon be coloured in, following European settlement or occupation. The Empire Road was born. But it was not tramped exclusively by British feet: adventurers from

Germany, Belgium, Portugal, France, Italy and Spain also lined up at the starting tape for the scramble for Africa.

Lesser, modern-day explorers have it easy. Of course, there is no lakeside road that will help me circumambulate the lake, but I will do my best to join the dots on my map in a general anti-clockwise fashion. I will also try to visit some smaller bodies of water in the Great Lake system: Lake Baringo, Lake Tanganyika, and the mysterious jade jewel, Lake Turkana, the largest desert lake in the world. As usual, I have no GPS, cellphone or laptop, but will rely on my trusted notepad, camera and voice recorder to document my experiences. Whatever didn't fit into my thirty-litre rucksack stuffed with a single change of clothes, was left behind.

What is it that has brought me here? Why have I returned to this continent for a third overland trip? Perhaps like the Maasai who must constantly follow their animals for the best grazing, I am heading for pastures new. New, but always Africa, the place with the greatest allure – the deep wells of sincerity, the harsh living, the wildlife, the capacity to see nothing as ordinary, an amazed attitude to life, and the open-armed hospitality all encourage exploration. Despite all the difficulties of travelling, there is something addictive about the continent in the same way that one never gets tired of looking at something flawed. Flawed and beautiful. African journeys have become a kind of seeing that puts all I know into a new, lucid light. By comparison, other places are all arriving and no travelling.

And why a bike? I come to immerse myself in unfamiliar ways of living, yet use what is the quintessential loner's vehicle. There are few experiences more revealing than riding an unfamiliar road to bring clarity to one's place in the world – and isn't that what we're all looking for? I may or may not find it around Lake Victoria.

Although I travel solo (Livingstone also disliked travelling with white men, finding them impatient and argumentative), I am never really alone because some things come with me that I don't pack – mostly the experiences of past journeys. Memories of previous trips and hopes for the new one coil together like a rope from which to climb the myths of the continent once more. Every return reminds me that the world is still full of wonder. Hopeful. Optimistic. And if you're not travelling optimistically, very little travelling is being done.

Now, two years after my last trip, I find one thing has led to another like the inevitability of a familiar tune, and I am back in the place of my dreams. T. E. Lawrence once wrote, "All men dream: but not equally." That's true: dreams in Africa are big and, personally speaking, more fully accommodate my life, like having an extra room to live in.

African travel is also an ache, albeit a pleasant one – but don't expect ever to be relieved. At home, the ache is kept at bay, hidden behind other thoughts. But it's always there, until I recognise it for what it is: the fuel for the next journey, like a promise waiting to be kept.

For now, while I keep my promise, the world can get on without me.

2

A SHIMMERING MOVEMENT OF COLOUR

Fired by the fugitive moment of escape, the following morning I eagerly search for the Thika Road, but I cannot see one signpost pointing north. Instead I accidentally veer into Kibera, the largest ghetto in Africa, where a million or more people swarming the roads and pavements, such as they are, seem intent on hampering my progress.

It's true what they say: there is no idleness in a slum. I am engulfed by swarms of delivery moto riders who believe I am there to race. Trucks with no side mirrors carrying everything from cupboards to cattle unknowingly push me off the road, while female point-duty cops blow whistles at me whether I go, stop, turn left, right or stall the bike in the middle of a crossroads. I never knew so much emotion could be transmitted through a whistle's pea.

Helpful men driving flatbed cars and vans flash headlights and wave me down.

'What do you do here?' they call urgently. 'What do you seek?'

When I tell them, they gesticulate wildly with scoops of laughter.

'You will not locate your road in Kibera,' says a driver. 'Only inconvenience!'

Eventually I find a closed slip road and slalom my way past a road gang, ride onto the Thika highway, the only multi-lane motorway in the country, and escape the city. Infrastructure development is always welcome in Africa, but I don't think the builders have thought everything through. Every few kilometres, in towns that have been cut in half by speeding vehicles, there is a zebra crossing painted on a speed bump across eight lanes of traffic. People who ignore the occasional newly constructed overhead walkway take their chances dodging the traffic. The first person onto the crossing is a brave Kenyan indeed.

The weather starts chilly but warms through the day as I head north. I am still at 1,600 metres altitude, so the real heat won't begin until I ride down from the Central Highlands. After a couple of hours inhaling truck fumes, I stop to stretch my legs at a roadside stall set up by Del Monte, the fruit company that owns most of the vast orchards in the region. It seems strange that locals would pay inflated prices for a ring-pull tin of fruit eaten directly out of the can with a cocktail stick rather than pick up the fresh version on the roadside. More than that, we are surrounded by the stuff: there are bananas and pineapples to every horizon.

Closer to Thika, I stop again when I see an old woman selling fruit on a homemade table. Before her is an immense bunch of just-picked bananas, large and small. I choose a bunch of tiny fat ones, each the size of my thumb.

The squatting woman looks up at me and says, 'Ten bob' (10 shillings, about 8p).

She sees the famished look on my face as I eat each one whole, so she gives me a bunch of longer bananas for comparison. I would be surprised if anyone in this parish goes hungry.

I check into a cheap hotel in Nyeri and go off to find Paxtu, the last home of Lord Baden-Powell, which is situated in the grounds of the pleasant Outspan Hotel. Baden-Powell was not only the founder of the Boy Scout movement, he was also a decorated soldier and Africaphile. During his lifetime he was more widely known for his army service throughout the British colonies: in the Zulu and Boer Wars in South Africa (most famously for the defence of the town at the Siege of Mafeking); in the fourth Ashanti War in the Gold Coast, present-day Ghana; and in India.

He first visited East Africa in 1906 as a war hero and returned to live here in 1939. His bestselling book, *Scouting for Boys*, which was a rewrite of his earlier military manuals used by the British Army to train local scouts, had already been published by this time. About four million copies of the UK edition have been sold, and roughly 100 million worldwide.

On Baden-Powell's instructions, the owner of the Outspan built a small hut in the hotel grounds in sight of Mount Kenya to the north-east. Calling the little cottage 'Paxtu', for peace, Baden-Powell and his wife spent the last two years of his life here. I was expecting something much grander for a baron's retirement villa, but today the hut is still no more than that. One of the two tiny rooms is open to the public and displays scouting memorabilia donated from scout troops around the world.

The owners of the hotel also built the more famous Treetops in Aberdare National Park about twenty kilometres away, the treehouse hotel where Princess Elizabeth heard that her father King George VI had died and that she had acceded to the throne.

I ride back to Nyeri, ten minutes away, but a world apart. People on the street have a new look. Many have darker skin, curious eyes and square foreheads more commonly seen in Somalia. Nyeri is probably the most colourful town I have ever visited. Building fronts are painted yellow, mauve, orange and emerald green. Double-story hand-painted advertisements spread like graffiti over walls, assaulting passers-by: "Nestle Milo Keeps Champions Going!", "G-Tide: Touch Me, Touch the World", "Earlybird Hotel", "Fanta – Bubbly and Irresistible".

Along the kerbstone is handwritten in white paint, "Discipline, Integrity, Sustainability, Customer Satisfaction, Operational Efficiency", which sounds like a mission statement from the local Chamber of Commerce and wholly appropriate for this bustling town.

I eat at the Town View restaurant, a name that exposes a local talent for exaggeration: the view from my seat looks directly out onto the concrete awning of the petrol station next door. Everybody in the dining room eats mutton curry and rice. The meat is almost inedible and I struggle to chew and swallow a single piece. I don't know what these people use for teeth.

I while away the evening idly watching a small flickering television, which is set high up on the bar. The news is a roll-call of the desperate and the worrying. There is a report on the latest crime statistics, which claim there are 600,000 illicit arms in Kenya, some of which are used in the eleven daily carjackings in Nairobi. There's no mention of bikejackings. Then the broadcast moves on to international stories. But I am not moved by the monumental news in the world; I am already more interested in the seemingly inconsequential things that line my day: the food on my plate, the petrol in my tank, the road surface under my wheels.

The programme ends when a weather girl, dressed so loudly that she could brighten up the cloudiest morning, says, 'Have a good night and a blessed day tomorrow.'

Let's hope so.

Next day I ride through recently harvested wheat fields as big as an English county and pass vast greenhouses growing flowers for the European market. Closer to the road, within inches of the speeding traffic, village women grow potatoes on freshly hoed verges, which are then sold by the bucket at the edge of the tarmac. Mount Kenya stays on my right as I make my way slowly around its west flank. Two hours later, halfway around the base of the mountain, I stop at the equator. I am approached by a man who wants to pour water from a jug into a bowl on both sides of the line to prove the opposing effects of gravity in each hemisphere. Or more accurately, he wants to relieve me of some money to perpetuate a scientific myth. He gives up on me and slopes back into a shop.

Further on, I stop in Nanyuki, a market town that serves both the busy farms in the area and the British Army base a few kilometres further up the road. The camp is perfectly placed for jungle training exercises on the mountain, and desert manoeuvres to the north. I know I've reached a place that serves Westerners, when a café waiter asks if I would like cappuccino rather than the more common freeze-dried Nescafé.

I read a remarkable but sad story in *The Daily Nation* about a woman who has given birth to six sets of twins. She has become a victim of her own fertility because her community believes she is cursed, and that one twin from each pair should be killed to ensure the survival of the other. Her life is in danger too. As a Bukusu, part of the Luhya tribe, friends and relations have all turned their backs on her and her seven daughters and five sons. The village elders want her to undergo a set of rituals, which includes washing her hair in goat's urine to cleanse her of bad spirits. She refuses because, as a converted Christian, she doesn't recognise the practice. To escape persecution she has moved into an orphanage with most of her children. Although I have only travelled 200 kilometres from Nairobi, reading this story makes me feel a long way from the city.

Once I leave the road that circles the base of Mount Kenya and head north into the lowlands, the heat builds. For the first time in Kenya I feel the sun reflecting off the tarred road. Eye-squinting vistas open up, and I can see hazy mountains in the landscape to the west like molehills in a meadow. In the foreground the wide plain is dotted with flat-topped acacia trees where starlings and weavers build well-crafted nests. They don't have to go far for material. The tracks to the rag-tag settlements further into the bush are marked along the road by little knots of boda-bodas waiting to pick up passengers who are dropped by *matatus*, the ubiquitous shared taxis that ply the main routes.

Just beyond the Jesus, Mary and Joseph Nomadic Rehab Centre I spot something up ahead near the top of a long incline. It looks like another ramshackle roadside stall selling vegetables or fruit – an odd place to wait for passing trade. As I get closer I am surprised to see that a moto, loaded with two man-sized charcoal sacks full of cabbages, has toppled over. Its rider, wearing a fleece and oversized trousers, is doing his best to lift the bike, but it is too much for one man. I park up and lend a hand. His antiquated bike is dressed with a tasselled blue tank cover, tasselled indicator lights and a home-made carry box fitted to the handlebars. These items are probably fitted to distract the eye from the obvious: the machine is a complete and utter wreck. And the tyres are flat.

'There is no starter,' says the rider. 'We must jump it.'

Even with two of us it is difficult to get the bike up off the ground. He then swings a leg over the seat and I throw my weight over the hundred or so cabbages to help balance the load. He manages it.

'Push!' he yells.

Push? I can hardly keep the thing upright.

'Push only!'

'But you're facing uphill!' I say.

'Push, I say!'

I suggest he turn to face downhill so that we can get the bike rolling before jump-starting the engine. But he doesn't want to lose any of the ground he has made towards town.

'*Push!*'

He leans against the bars as I push with all my weight against the cabbages, and we somehow manage to move the bike two metres, which is enough for the motor to catch. He screams the revs in appreciation and, with only a breath of air in both tyres, lollops off over the crest of the hill.

I get on my bike and soon overtake him; ten kilometres on I stop at the bottom of the long, straight road to take a picture of the impressive landscape. I hear the wheel rims scraping on the tarmac before I see the cabbage rider. He whooshes past – freewheeling with a dead engine.

'You need help?' he calls.

Before I can answer, he shouts, 'Can't stop!'

Forty kilometres on, I reach Isiolo, a big step towards my immediate goal of Lake Turkana. The town is a treat for the senses, and I see it all through a swirl of dust and sand; even the other side of the street seems far away. Squatting men with dyed-orange beards and hair make deals as they throw nuts into their mouths like tossing dice. A few Somalis walk past, tall and graceful with matted hair, wearing robes or too-short suits that belong on a scarecrow. Three young would-be race-car drivers rowdily push home-made toy cars the size of large dogs down the road.

Close to a noisy posho mill (corn mill), I check into the Jabal-Nur Plaza, 'The Mountain of Light'. If only. The place is a dark pit. The open shower-cum-shithole is one metre from the head of the bed and the toilet door, permanently swung open, is rotting with years of misdirected piss.

I bring the bike into the little courtyard that is flapping with laundry. Two men confront me.

'You will leave the moto here?' asks one.

'Yes. Shouldn't I?'

They exchange significant looks.

The barefoot man says, 'You know there are people who will take this bike.'

'From the courtyard?'

'Why not? Other guests! You must be fearful.'

Perhaps I should start by being a little wary of these two who seem unusually interested in the details of the bike.

'And what is this?' asks the other, bending down to inspect the beatbox.

'A radio.'

'A radio! It is too easy to lose a radio in this place.'

I park the bike in such a way that I can see it if I poke my head out of the first floor room I have been given. When the two men lose interest and drift away, I unload my gear and take it up to my room. The door next to mine is open and the barefoot man is inside lying on a bed, the only item of furniture I can see.

'You are staying at the hotel?' I ask.

'I live here,' he says. 'I am security.'

Within an hour I have scoffed a plate of *nyama choma*, goat meat in gravy. I then take a place on the step of a walkway in front of a row of shops, a prime spot from which to weigh up the virtues of Isiolo. The place teems with its own versions of life. Most of the town seems to get about on embellished boda-bodas that sport tassels in the unlikeliest places or hand-painted fairings, tanks and mirrors. Old women riding pillion skid past, gripping their shopping, while schoolchildren and squinting men with holes in their earlobes the size of a 50p coin disappear into the dust. Others hold on to their *kufi* caps with waistcoats buttoned up over robes, as makeshift neckerchiefs tug in the wind. Schoolgirls in spotless white headscarves leave the mosque and walk home in tight huddles. Others in emerald green uniforms and satchels on their backs clash with another class of kids wearing dark blue cardigans and crested badges on breast pockets. Boda-boda riders without a fare sit sideways on their bikes under a tree, Henry-style.

A teenager leaves the Jamhuri Guest House – its motto, "Life's Full of Flavour" – and joins me on the step. It should help me to blend in a little if I look like I have a reason to be here. The boy questions me about my destination, the top speed of the bike, how I am coping in the heat.

'This is not Nairobi,' he says, as if I need reminding.

He is surprised that I should come here now because tensions in the town have been simmering for a while.

He says, 'A lot of people have been killed between tribes. There has been conflict for months. The desert people, the nomads, they fight. It is dangerous for them out in the desert, so they come to Isiolo. Many have no homes after they were burned. But you can see...' he indicates, looking up and down the street, 'it is a mix of people. These shops here were closed for days, weeks, because of the fighting.'

'When was this?'

'This year. And for many years before.'

I scan the roadside and become aware that the men around us are quiet – so quiet that I can only hear women's voices. The men watch, creating an airtight atmosphere. They are watching each other. A small cluster of Turkana men in cast-off Western clothing chew the *miraa* leaf, a mild stimulant, which might account for the aggressively casual air.

Then I notice a blaze of colour: three women scuffing up puffballs of dust move towards us. They wear straps of multicoloured beads around their heads and calves, and countless more around their necks that weigh heavy on bare shoulders. Ears, too, are adorned with long, swinging trinkets and more beadwork. One wears a strip of beads from ear to ear that touches the point of her nose, and another strip that acts as a chin strap. Wedged into their headbands are trinkets, silver charms and colourful baubles.

'Where have these people come from?' I ask.

'Some are Samburu, some Turkana, some Borana,' says the teenager. 'From Lake Turkana. They come to buy from the shops. They will go back today, to the desert.'

The women bustle past with babies on their backs and full shopping bags. Talking loudly, they look neither left nor right as they make their way to a *matatu* stop. I know I am in a strange place when such a scene can go unremarked by all except me.

Then a woman in a business suit and heels steps unsteadily down the broken, dusty street, which now, after only two hours in Isiolo, is one of the most bizarre sights I have ever seen.

The following day I take the road north towards Marsabit, where I hope to find a track across the Chalbi Desert to South Horr and on to the southern tip of Lake Turkana. There are no cars on the road and only the occasional truck heading south. Soaring white hawks, flapping grey and yellow hornbills and stationary ostriches are the only company on the scorching road. Once, to the east, I see a kudu, the corkscrew-horned antelope common in these parts. I stop when I come across a traffic casualty in the centre of the road – a hyena. It is odd to see the menacing scavenger lying motionless next to a trickle of blood on the hot tarmac. There is no one about and I get a shiver being so close to the animal. I don't touch it in case it is not quite dead.

A little further on I stop to drink the last of my water and out of nowhere two Samburu appear, one a *moran*, the other a shaven-headed elder. The *moran*, topless and shiny-skinned, wears a cerise sarong and elaborate beading around his neck and wrists and diagonally across his chest. His long, plaited hair is ochre-stained. He has beaded earrings and wooden blocks wedged into his earlobes. He carries a herding staff and a *knobkerrie* (thick-ended club). They are both friendly and, using some elementary sign language, ask for a pen each. Then the warrior takes great care to write on his hand "ROMAS", an action that brings smiles from all three of us.

'Nice to meet you, Romas,' I say.

A young boy herding camels arrives. He speaks some English, so I tell him about the hyena.

'How far?' he asks with some urgency.

'Two or three kilometres,' I say.

The boy interprets for the others and all three run off down the road in the direction of the dead animal.

The encounter allays my apprehensions about the desert people that were stirred up by Henry in Nairobi, and I continue in a buoyant mood. That is more than I can say for the performance of the bike, which I have not yet mentioned, mainly because I have been hoping that if I ignored the problem it might go away. The intermittent putt-putt-putt of the engine sounds like Chitty Chitty Bang Bang. I have tried to disregard the stuttering that kicked in the second I left Nairobi, but I know it is not going to end well. After a week with the troublesome bike I know its workings like I know my own teeth: that is, I'm most aware of it when it gives me pain.

Further north, the bike splutters and coughs and feels very reluctant to reach Laisamis, the next town. By the time I arrive at the village of Sere Olupi I am having to coax the throttle like a sulky child. I shift down the gears and, now that the bike senses neutral, the engine dies as I freewheel off the road.

Somebody is roused from his slumber under a tree and helps me push the bike to the shade of a church hall, where we step back and look at it – me with disgust, him with curiosity. I can't help but notice that the man is a little unsteady on his feet, and wonder if he has a disability of some kind.

'There is a mechanic,' he says.

'Great.'

'But he is not here.'

Not so great.

He pulls out a few *miraa* leaves from his trouser pocket and pushes them into his mouth. The guy is not disabled, he's high.

He thinks for a second, sways a little, then says, 'It is okay. I will go for the doctor.'

'I'm fine,' I say. 'It's the bike that needs help.'

'The doctor will know a plan,' he says, and runs in zig-zags across the sand towards the main road as his friends cheer his unsteady progress.

Ten minutes later a middle-aged man arrives on a 250cc Yamaha, with the helpfully high man on pillion.

'You're the village doctor?' I ask.

'It is so,' he says.

He is not thrilled at being pulled away from no doubt more urgent matters to help a passing motorist, but his kindly attitude tells me that he will not leave a stranger stranded. He tries the starter, adjusts the choke, tries it again; then he pulls at something, pushes something else. There's only one thing I can say.

'What's the diagnosis, doctor?'

I will him to say something like, 'There's no time to lose. We've got to get this patient to the hospital right away.'

Instead, he looks at me impassively, and says, 'The spark plug. It is bad.'

He unscrews the plug. But as neither he nor I have another, he merely looks at it and screws it back in. He tries the starter again. The motor catches, but it's hesitant. There is now a crowd. We all stand around looking at the bike spluttering and wait for it to die again, as people do who have nothing to add. In the meantime, the doctor notices a missing screw on the right handlebar and takes it upon himself to remove an identical screw from the left bar to plug the gap on the right. Even I know that will make no difference to my progress down this road. Then, as often happens with intermittent mechanical problems, the engine rights itself and begins running sweetly. The doctor takes credit for the repair.

'Where do you go?' the doctor asks.

'Lake Turkana.'

'There is no petrol,' he says, flatly. 'Do you carry your own?'

I kick the can of fuel lashed to the side of the bike as an indication that I've thought of every eventuality.

'Good luck with your bike,' he says, unable to hide his derision, 'and your can of fuel.'

The break in my journey, coupled with the heat, has brought on a weariness. I've had a long day already so I ask if there is any food in the village.

The man who's away with the fairies says, 'We have, we have. We will take you.'

He and the doctor lead me to the village limit, where we ride up to a shack within sight of the road. I see nothing to indicate the presence of any food except six men slouching around an empty table in the shade. They have the haunted and tragic look of war casualties. The doctor and the helpful man leave.

I take a seat at the other table next to a covered bucket on the ground. The man who picked me up earlier might have been leathered, but these guys outside the shack are paralytic. In a gesture of welcome one man gets to his unsteady feet and tries to bow, which looks as if he's dancing. None can focus on me, but that doesn't stop a fiercely aggressive conversation ensuing about my presence. No matter what anybody says to me, another takes savage exception to it.

'Can I get something to eat?' I interrupt.

One of the men shouts something. An elderly woman arrives from around the back of the shack. She too is pie-eyed. She calls. A teenage girl who was clearly dozing twenty seconds ago comes out as she smoothes down her full-length skirt. She is blinking furiously – and also spaced.

'Do you have food?' I ask.

'I am not confused,' she answers, her voice thick with sleep.

I leave a pause, hoping she'll come around and realise which world she's in.

'Food?' I ask.

'*Githeri*,' she says.

The crowd of onlookers laugh.

'You know it?' she asks. 'Beans. And chapati.'

The girl removes the lid from the plastic bucket on the ground next to me. The foul-smelling beans are probably yesterday's leftovers not yet grown fully cold and congealing thickly. She scoops a plastic cupful and pours it onto a tin plate, then she drops three chapatis on top and hands it to me. It's so high, it's practically fermenting. The only way not to smell it is to eat it, which is like consuming somebody else's sick. My dining companions are encouraging and enjoy the sight of the food disappearing inside me, except for the man on his feet who now looks like he's doing Tai Chi with his heels nailed to the floor. He levels a stream of nonsensical words in my direction that sounds like a tape cassette playing backwards.

Somehow I eat half the beans and two chapatis. The man with the loose legs returns and I use the interruption as an excuse to leave. I pay the girl who is now slumped on the ground, then give him 100 shillings for his help.

'Don't spend it all on *miraa*!' I say.

'No. I have plenty,' he says, pulling a fistful of fresh leaves out of his pocket.

3

THE WATER CARRIER

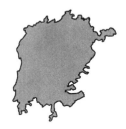

The little roadside village turns out to have been a convenient place to rest because it marked the end of the tarred road. The new surface is all jagged rocks and corrugations and is making mincemeat of the little bike, which returns to its fit of hiccups every time I slip into fourth gear. The doctor's remedy was only a temporary treatment until I can find a specialist.

The afternoon sun turns brutal as I move into a semi-desert landscape of low, spindly trees and dust devils that shift in columns across my path. After suffering the burning hours of the afternoon and the torturous road surface, I stop, shaken to the core, in a little community of dwellings the shape of large igloos. The homes are made from sticks, blankets and sacks, and look as if they have come to rest after a hurricane. Perhaps these are the nomads that the boy mentioned in Isiolo. I see a sign that says, "Nabosu bar, restaurant and lodging. Well-Come".

Two men walk towards me down the centre of the road, so I wait for them to arrive. Without the breeze of movement, sweat pours out of me like water through a strainer.

'What's the road ahead like?' I ask.

The younger says, 'It is bad.' Indicating the rough surface, he adds, 'This will be tarmac one day, so the road from South Africa to Ethiopia will be tarred. But for now it is like this.'

I check the time.

'Will I make it to the next village before dark?'

'It is possible. But on this bike?' He shrugs.

'Point taken,' I say.

The man, who introduces himself as Bosco, says, 'Make a decision. Do not do nothing. The road is no better ahead. We have lodging and food. If you go to the next village you will have no services.'

That settles it.

'Where can I spend the night?' I ask.

He points to a metal gate, which gives access to a small compound with a row of cinder block rooms behind blue doors. I push open the gate and see a girl scrubbing the colour out of a shirt, and another hanging bed sheets on a line. One kicks open a blue door, which reveals a bed and mosquito net. It's bare but the empty room is more welcoming than the Jabal-Nur Plaza, and there is a strong possibility of some clean sheets.

'I'll take it.'

I collapse on the bed and am asleep before I'm able to take off my boots.

I am not sure what disturbs me, but when I wake I notice that someone has opened the door. I am less concerned with who might have come into the room than with the images beyond the threshold. In my half-sleep I am transfixed by a shimmering movement of colour. Through the opening, beyond the chicken wire fence and deep into the heat haze, I see two streams of fantastically dressed women: one stream moves uphill, the other down, elegant and purposeful. The women walking downhill are quiet and lope a measured stride with heads bowed, while those heading uphill are chatty and gay. Water carriers!

I leave the room and walk up towards the shallow incline where there is a scene at the water pump. About forty women and children jostle for water that is pouring out of two faucets attached to a standpipe. They fight to hold their plastic containers, jugs, bottles and jerry cans under the splashing water, but they also laugh as they stagger in the slippery sand. There are no men.

The women and girls are other-worldly. They do not walk as you and I might walk. When they move they jingle and sway; it is as if they bring with them not just their bodies but their lives, their histories. The women have partially shaved heads and wear red or tartan blankets, yellow wraps or layered sarongs and sandals. Their headdresses are constructed around closely woven headbands decorated with buttons and flimsy metal trinkets dangling front-centre over their foreheads. Others have headdress weights with hanging baubles that shake. Dozens of bangles that have been forced through their ears rattle and shake, beads hang through pierced lips and dangle on the chin, scores of multicoloured bead necklaces hang loose around necks and over shoulders, ankles are wrapped in red, yellow, orange and blue beads.

Some women have bird feathers stuck in headbands like mohawks. Others wear black and red striped tops that hang loose, showing small, lively breasts. Some pubescent girls have raw welts on their bodies from fresh scarification, and wear tight gold bangles on the upper arms and silver bracelets on wrists. A few have weights in their ears that stretch lobes unnaturally, almost touching their shoulders.

You may now have a colourful picture in your mind's eye – but imagine seeing this vision after waking up in the semi-desert with sand and dust rising in the air, against the backdrop of an ill-defined horizon and poker-red setting sun. Sometimes the reality can be more dreamlike than the memory, for I know I cannot recreate fully what I am seeing. It is the first time on the journey that even though I may be a long way from home, I know it is where I ought to be.

The beauty of the moment is made more so by the fact that the women are here for the purest reason: water. Simple, running water. They have come with twenty-five-litre jerry cans and plastic food containers with rags for stoppers. They come with babies on their backs or in their bellies, and sometimes both. One teenager, whose child is surely her first, carries two square containers by thick handles; another feeds a looped length of cloth through the handle, swings it onto her lower back and wraps the cloth around her forehead before staggering off.

The younger children, nakedly innocent and beautiful, play in the mud and pick and throw garbage because it's the most fascinating thing to do. Until, that is, I arrive.

The first woman that sees me asks for 100 shillings for a photograph. White people have been here before. I neither give her money nor take a photo, but I think I can be more useful. I pick a woman at random and, using sign language, offer to pick up the water.

'Let me help you,' I say.

The suggestion catches and lights up several faces. I can now see that many women have prominent front teeth, which are streaked with discolouration. They cackle and backslap each other, before a woman points to the largest jerry can brimming with water with a plastic bag wedged into the top.

I have not yet heard English spoken here, but there is one woman in Western dress.

'Where to?' I ask.

She says, 'The child will show you.'

A shaven-headed girl of about eight looks up at me.

'Where?' I ask.

She points down past the lodging compound towards the mud huts on the far side of the village. I pick up the can. Good God. What have I done. I have just offered to carry twenty-five kilograms of water to the furthest point of the village. I hesitate and look around once more. All the children point down the village. Then they look up at me as if I am about to jump out of an aeroplane without a parachute, so fantastical is the notion that a white man should carry water. At least it's slightly downhill.

I pick up the can by the greasy handle and head down the path. The children scream as one and run to their mothers. Then they get more inquisitive and trail after me, keeping their distance but still close enough to be part of this extraordinary spectacle. I have to rest half a dozen times on the way, but I eventually make it. The eight-year-old opens the door of the hut and the foul sweetness of the interior hits me as I pour the water into a barrel. A quick look inside tells me they have nothing to spare.

'One!' I say.

'ONE!' they all say.

'We go again.'

A ripple goes around the kids. *I don't believe it, he's going back for more!*

I walk back up to the water pump with my posse in tow.

I ask the woman in Western clothing, 'Why is the whole village here at the same time?'

'The water is turned on only once a week. So we all come. If you do not come now you do not get water!'

'Why is that?'

'They switch it on and off,' she says, gesturing towards a "World Vision" sign 100 metres away.

'But it is better. Last year we had drought and no water at all.'

I catch the eye of a woman with metre-long loops of beads through her ears and deep scarification marks on her cheeks.

'Shall I carry for you?' I ask.

As soon as I pick up the can the children point to another part of the village. The can is a bit lighter, so the journey isn't such a trial of strength, but still women carrying larger water containers on their heads overtake me without a murmur. I reach the second hut and some of the kids squeal with delight.

'Two!'

'TWO!'

On the walk back to the pump I pick up a dead snake and the bleached skull of a goat and chase the children with them. I am slowly winning them over – and the women. They are less shy each time I return. But strangely, even though there is always a full can ready to be carried to a distant dwelling, I get precious little thanks for my efforts. The English speaker passes critical/ironic/hilarious comment to the women at the pump on every pass. Once, she translates: 'We think you are getting tired!' There is challenge rather than empathy in her tone.

Determinedly, I pick up another jerry can, which causes the women to whoop and howl with their hands on their knees. *The water run has rarely been so remarkable.*

Occasionally, I encounter men on my treks. They greet me modestly, but must be thinking, *What a bloody fool, doing women's work.*

And so it continues for the next hour until, sweating and gasping, I reach a hut, no more than a temporary shelter, and leave the can next to the open fire inside. I feel immense.

'Fourteen!' I call, almost breathless.

'FOURTEEN!' shout the kids who haven't left my side all evening.

Later, I take a scalding shower in water that's been boiling in the sun all day in a rooftop oil drum. Then I head out to look for food. The only place with any movement is the Nabosu Complex bar: after dark it's just a candlelit cinder block building selling beer to dark figures slumped in corners. The only woman in the place is behind the counter.

I ask, 'Is there anything to eat?'

'No food.'

I want to ask what the "Complex" bit of the name refers to, but instead I settle for a bottle of Serengeti beer.

A voice says, 'Buy me beer, man.'

A man in the half-light kicks over a chair and repeats, 'Buy me a beer.'

He is drunk, and the situation has quickly become confrontational.

'I've only enough for one,' I say.

The man stands up, unsteady on his feet, but still a lot taller than me. Then, as if by appointment, Bosco arrives at the door.

'Come sit with us,' he says. 'She will bring the beer.'

The drunk man snorts and flops back into his seat. Bosco leads me outside beyond the rectangle of light coming from the bar, where a circle of men sit on white plastic chairs. In the darkness I hear bits of broken conversation and can just make out the moonshine on their clammy faces, which are turned towards the stars. The men nearest to me wear Western clothing and have the look of the utterly exhausted.

'We meet every month,' says Bosco. 'We are a club. Pleased for you to be here.'

'What kind of club?'

If he'd asked me to guess, I'd still be guessing now.

'A Catholic club,' he says.

'Catholics? In the desert?'

'There are only a few in this region,' Bosco says. 'There are Italian priests in some villages. It is true! I am the headteacher of the primary school.'

I shake everybody's hand and then Bosco insists on stacking three chairs so that my seat is sturdier than theirs.

'Do you have all that you need?' he asks.

'I could use some food.'

'There is no food in the Complex but you may have what we ate earlier. We watched you when you carried your water, but you were so serious we did not invite you! Was I right to do it?'

I laugh, and the bizarre nature of the late afternoon comes back to me.

The man on my left is the bar owner. He calls for a girl who brings me the men's scraps from a goat that Bosco cooked earlier this evening. A cloud moves in front of the moon and it becomes so dark that I cannot see my hands, let alone what is on my plate. I pick out what I can. I'm putting all sorts into my mouth – bone, gristle, rancid fat. Then Bosco points a torch at the food as I feed the last of the leftover goat into my startled gullet.

When I have finished, he drops the torch and closes his eyes. I feel the evolution of the day and allow myself to enjoy the deeper intimacy of the night. The men gossip as if planning tomorrow's battle. After forty minutes, Bosco drifts off into tiredness or drunkenness before shaking himself awake and heading home. I take the opportunity to get another beer from the bar. The belligerent locals are still making a nuisance of themselves, but there is another teacher at the bar, a man dressed in clothes that still have the creases.

I tell him my plan to find a route across the desert to Lake Turkana. His face puckers.

'You are in a 4x4?'

'Bike.'

'In a team?'

'Just me.'

'You cannot carry enough fuel for the trip. It cannot be done,' he says, encouraging no more discussion.

'How far is it?'

'I do not know. It is not a route that we take. The desert is not as good as this road.'

'This road' is a bone-jarring nightmare, so the desert track must be a scream. I checked the map earlier and it seemed to show that the lake is no more than 180 kilometres away, which at ten kilometres per litre of petrol is just within the range of the bike. But of course that does not allow for the sandy track, and the windy route, and getting lost.

'There is no fuel along the way,' he says. 'The Samburu have no need for vehicles or petrol. They are desert people.'

I push him. 'Can it be done? Can I get to Lake Turkana?'

He turns more positive. 'Anything can be achieved with determination. Even by a *mzungu*. Perhaps if you leave by five o'clock before the sun rises. If not, you will regret it.'

I order the teacher another beer, but I call it a night. I step back outside into the blackness. The men from the Catholic club have all gone home, and it is now so dark I feel as though I could touch it. The worry for the trip ahead swells up in me, but here in the dark at least I do not have to worry about showing it.

By instinct alone I find my room, where there is somebody sleeping on a straw mattress across my door. The curled figure, snoring loudly, is covered by a mosquito net, which is held up by a tie that is wrapped around my window catch. I manage to get inside without waking him. He snores through the whole night.

4

THE DESERT

I wake to thoughts already energised by the blood of expectation. I am ready to leave by 6 a.m. The man sleeping guard outside my door turns out to be the owner of the Nabosu Complex bar. I pay him for the room, then ride further up the road to a small row of shops. I order breakfast: eggs, *mandazi* (sweet doughnuts) and *chai* – sweet, milky tea.

I ask the cook, 'Where can I buy petrol?'

'Here. I have it.'

He returns with two five-litre disinfectant bottles full of fuel. I finish my breakfast and the man follows me out to the bike.

As he fills my tank, he says, 'Lake Turkana? It is far. Maybe too far.'

He then tops up my jerry can to the brim.

'You will need all your fuel,' which he pronounces *foo-ell*. Maybe it's not a mispronunciation.

'You will meet the warriors,' he says, 'but do not stop for them. Keep going. There have been aggressions in the past.'

'With *mzungus*?'

'Between themselves,' he says. 'For land. That is why they carry weapons.'

This is getting more serious.

'Guns?' I ask.

'Guns, yes, and spears or sticks,' he says. 'Keep going. Do not stop.'

'Will they give me trouble?'

He ignores my question. 'Head for Ngurunit,' he says. 'There will be only you. There are many forks, many ways.'

As the sun rises, I ride out beyond the village limit and reach a track heading north-west. Yesterday these temporary dwellings were beyond mainstream society. Now, in my rear view mirror, they look like the perimeter of something important.

The road surface changes from a comical shuddering over rocks and through potholes to a barely controllable glide over sand that has already lost its sheen of morning dew. As the sun warms the earth it quickly feels like the middle of the day. There are no tyre tracks on the route, just a few windblown footprints. After half an hour the track is dry and powdery as chalk. I reach a rocky section and then some very deep sand that slows me to a crawl. I'm in first gear but it still feels as though I could lose the bike from under me at any moment.

There are no signs. The way is marked by scrubby bush and the occasional low tree; mostly it's sand as far as I can see. Every kilometre, the way is emptier. Empty of people, empty of man-made intrusions, empty of green. When you don't have green, you miss it. The silence races through me and I have the feeling that I've left something behind, as if I have cast off without a vital piece of equipment. Rather than get nearer, in my mind's eye I see Ngurunit receding into the distance.

I reach a bridge that has collapsed with no obvious alternative route to the other side of a deep, dry riverbed. I retrace my track to the last fork and take the other option. Soon I see an elderly couple walking towards me. I stop, but they take defensive action by stepping off the trail and hiding behind a tree. I yell over to them to ask if this is the correct way for Ngurunit, which must come across as a hostile gesture. Although they remain silent, they smile kindly, probably in the hope that I will move quickly past. Further on, I pass some young boys herding goats who beg aggressively for money. I am only going 20 kph so the kids don't give up easily, and follow me down the track until they get bored.

Soon after, I see three *morani*, the warriors that Henry warned me about. They are wearing red face paint and red and yellow tartan sarongs. Their hair is braided and dyed red. Two hold spears, the third a thick club. I approach slowly. I have no choice in this terrain. Rather than flick the wrist as beggars do, they hold out both hands. Then I see that they are not begging but rather flexing their taught chests, which are adorned with deep scarification marks. Intricate necklaces of beads and flimsy metal trinkets drape around their shoulders. The brilliant costumes set against their black skin below the blue sky is arresting, but most of all it is their physiques that are most striking. Their arms are wrapped in tight charm bracelets that emphasise bulging biceps. Their skin is smooth: not worn smooth but chiselled and buffed like statues, to be admired as much as feared. My world shrinks to the width of my seat.

I get closer and wave, 'Hello!'

I get nothing back.

'Ngurunit?'

Not a flicker.

'Lake Turkana?'

I become aware that I'm sweating drinks I had last night, and my awkward, ill-fitting body feels in the way. I am upon them and the three men reluctantly step off the track at the last second, so as not to be struck by a wing mirror. They utter guttural sounds, which I take to be threats. The moment I am past, I flinch slightly, expecting to be hit by something. I bend down to look in the mirror and realise that one is running alongside the bike, swishing the air with a club. I want to get away but the more I twist the throttle, the more the back wheel spins, and the slower I go. I must keep a cool head. He shouts something that startles me and the bike squirms in the sand. Everything in me is willing the bike to remain upright and moving.

'I have nothing!' I shout. Which I admit, from this distance, sounds a ridiculous thing to say to a desert man when you're riding through his land on a new motorbike with a rucksack on the back.

I catch his eye as he swings the heavy end of the club. It clips me on the shoulder before hitting me square on the side of my helmet. The time for words, however inane, is over. *Keep upright.* I am soon twenty metres down the track and he gives up. Although I am delighted to be past this hurdle, I am already worrying about the next obstacle.

I am right to be worried.

Further on I come across more young boys herding. Rather than come towards me, they retreat and pick up heavy rocks in defensive poses. Then there are more *morani*, keen to show that they do not cower from a *mzungu* on a moto, by making me ride through a gauntlet of ready spears. The attitude seems to be getting more aggressive, the further I am from the road. I begin to feel less like a traveller, and more like a trespasser – but I have invested so much of my future imagination in this venture in the desert that somehow I find it in myself to continue.

After four tough hours I stop in a dry riverbed and kill the engine. The silence hurts my ears and now that I have stopped moving, a sense of scale hits me. Since I left Laisamis there have been no markers, no vehicles, nobody in Western clothing, no water, no supplies of any kind. I'm out there. I assess my position which, without a GPS, is frankly impossible. Apart from knowing I have not yet reached Ngurunit, I don't know where the fuck I am.

Half a day in, I'm losing my grip on why I have come this distance, and I recognise the journey has acquired a new seriousness. How important is it to reach Lake Turkana? Not one person I have met speaks English, to the extent that they cannot even understand my pronunciation of Lake Turkana, so what chance do I have to find the correct track with so many forks on the route? I am almost at the point where I don't think I will be able to retrace my steps, should I choose to turn back. In fact, I may have reached that point already. Am I likely to meet more Samburu warriors further down the track? Clearly, yes. Are they likely to be more welcoming to Westerners? I don't think I need to answer that question.

I get off the bike and look back down the track. The trail of the tyre mark in the sand is at once a beguiling and terrifying sight. My mind has only one thought: turn back. This is the place where the road runs out of patience with me. I drink half my water in one go and decide to act. Rather than continue into the unknown, I'll return and take my chances with the *morani* I have already passed.

An hour later, I reach a familiar long stretch of deep sand, at the end of which I see the three warriors. I feel like Gary Cooper in *High Noon*. There is no alternative route; I have to ride to them, past them, through them maybe. As I come within thirty metres, one takes his spear by its end and aims it at me. He then shrieks something that puts the fear of God into all believers and non-believers within earshot, but I know I cannot stop – not now. Another *moran* puts out his hand as if to grab the handlebar. I unzip my tank bag and take out the half-full bottle of water. The man holding the spear steps to one side, to get a better swing? I am only moving at 15 kph; he could push me off at this speed. I hold out the bottle, which seems to distract him for a second and he transfers the spear to his other hand. He takes the bottle.

'It's yours!' I say.

He yells again. Whatever it was, it wasn't 'Thank you kindly.'

The ground firms up and I get a little traction on the back tyre, but I soon notice a shadow running on the ground beside me. One of the *morani* is keeping up with the bike, even though I get up some speed. I feel the pressure to give in. *Not now.*

'I already gave!' I shout. My comments are getting more ridiculous.

He pokes his spear into the spokes of the front wheel and I brace myself for a fall – but as the wheel turns, the suspension fork snaps off the end of the spear and he gives up. I'm away. I'm gripping the seat between my legs like a vice, but I'm away. I realise I have not taken a breath since I gave the bottle, and now the relief sends my pulse into convulsions.

All I need do now is find my route back to the road. I am on edge until I reach the collapsed bridge, when I know I am as good as home. Metre by metre I sense familiarity in the scene, and follow my track as though it is the road from Narnia back to the wardrobe.

I know I have come through something, and am thrilled when I reach the previously despised Marsabit road. I ride through Laisamis without stopping, and keep going for another hour to put some distance between me and the embarrassment of the desert track. And the *morani.*

When the rough road turns to tarmac, I stop for a breather. I sit with a group of idle men who find new depths of amusement in the fact that I turned tail in the desert. I am left with the feeling that something important happened this morning, that I am changed in some way. A lesson learned. It might take some time to discover exactly what that is.

Then the man who sold me petrol shows up on a motorbike. He is not surprised to hear my story.

He says, 'You did a good thing to return. I say a prayer for you after you left this morning.'

Looking back, I had little going for me. It was a ridiculous notion to cross the desert without a more detailed map, especially when the place is riddled with locals who see intimidation of a lone *mzungu* on a Chinese bike as some kind of warrior rite of passage.

I was to undergo two final indignities this morning. Twenty minutes later on the tarred road I pass three men, one a traditionally dressed *moran*. I give them a wide berth, but as soon as I am level with them, one throws a rock the size of a melon at the bike. It misses. I am relieved, and feel as though the chase is over. However, the lonely road south is not yet finished with me.

I see three trucks heading north on the Isiolo road all day, the last of which waves me down. He puts on his warning lights as he approaches on a long straight. I deduce that he must be warning me about an obstacle or some danger up ahead.

I slow to a crawl and shout, 'What's happening?'

He doesn't reply. We pass and he stops just behind me. The driver jumps down from the cab and calls me over. I U-turn and ride towards him as he walks up to me on the shimmering tarmac. Something about the little scene strikes me as incongruent. For a start it's thirty-five degrees and he's wearing a bomber jacket zipped up tight. He gets closer with a worrying spring in his step and I see that his hands are fisted deep in his side pockets.

'What's up?' I ask, still astride my bike.

'My friend,' he says. 'I need help.'

'What's wrong?'

I get a little suspicious, so I U-turn again to face the way I was going. He is now walking towards me behind my right shoulder.

When he is nearly upon me, he says, 'How far to Laisamis?'

There is no way a truck driver would not know the distance to the next town. He looks left and right, up and down the road. Then his eyes lock onto the bike's ignition key. I ride off five metres.

He repeats, 'Laisamis?'

'Eighty kilometres,' I say.

'Come here!' he calls.

He unzips his jacket and thrusts his hand inside. The air is now loaded. Occasionally I fail to read the intentions of others, but not today. I don't want to be here when he pulls out whatever he's clutching in his jacket. Flooded with the anticipation of pain, I crouch down, squeeze the throttle while praying that the spark plug doesn't die, and leave like a bullet leaves a gun.

5

HOME OF CHAMPIONS

Sometimes a fresh beginning is no further than a tankful of petrol and a following wind. With the air blowing the smell of rain into my face, I ride from the desert back up to the Central Highlands, and soon have to put on all the clothes I possess to keep warm. It is Sunday, and Nanyuki is quiet. There is a restaurant on a corner that has some lights on, but the door is locked. A boda-boda rider sees my disappointment and bangs on the door until a white man answers. He says that if I buy beer, he will make me a plate of food.

Derek, three years out of Cornwall, is making a stack of pizzas for British troops, which will be delivered to the base twenty minutes away by the boda-boda waiting outside. Derek wants to talk, but I am still gathering up all the experiences from the desert and forming them into a hard ball in the pit of my stomach. As worrying as the incidents were, my travels seem to rely on such events to push me this way or that. What had only yesterday seemed real and threatening was already part of my imagination.

Next day I ride west on a road that takes me back off the highlands and cuts through conservancies and game reserves. The dirt road starts out broken-up tarmac, turns to rocks and then evens out to gravel, where I have to ride around lethargic camels grazing on the track. The scenes of wild grassland, little villages and picturesque hills deserve to be on a postcard. The conservancy wire fences separate me from zebra, giraffes, buck and elephants, the last of which (should they manage to flatten the fence) are prevented from straying too far by "Live Danglies", electrified elephant fences that swing from an overhead line at helmet level above the track.

When I reach Nyahururu, my destination for today, I sense the bike doesn't want to stop. The angry motor has temporarily calmed. Sometimes you have to trust inanimate objects to know things that you can't understand, so I keep going. Six kilometres before I reach Nakuru I stop at a viewpoint on the Laikipia Escarpment, a breathtaking route down into the Great Rift Valley, a geological feature on a scale with which few Europeans will be familiar. Six thousand kilometres long, the valley runs from Syria in the Middle East through Eritrea, Ethiopia, Kenya, Tanzania and ends in Mozambique in south-east Africa. It is not a river valley, but rather a series of geological trenches caused by movement of the Earth's crust. It links some of the world's deepest lakes and the earliest human fossils have been discovered here, giving rise to its epithet as the cradle of civilisation. From the roadside viewpoint it seems like I can see most of it.

The following day I head for the freshwater Lake Baringo, to the north. The ride, through a pastoral scene with hazy mountains in the middle distance, is like a private viewing in an aviary, such is the abundance of bird life. The region might lack manufacturers, but there is an industry about the people. The farms that grow long rows of aloes and sisal are thriving, and are surrounded by small herds of cattle and grazing goats. However, access to water seems to be a common problem, as I am regularly passed by moto riders carrying six twenty-five-litre jerry cans of water, making deliveries to remote communities.

That night I stay at a tented camp clinging to the edge of the lake. The staff tell me that the recent heavy rains have meant that they have lost more than half the camp ground in the last year because of the rise in water level. I take a cheap *banda* (basic thatched cabin), dump my gear, then walk to the water's edge, no more than forty paces away. I do a 360 with the video camera and when I scan over the lake surface about ten metres away, something unexpected moves in the viewfinder: a hippopotamus coming up for air, which yawns me a greeting.

There is constant activity in the trees: yellow-billed hornbills squawk above my cabin, African jacanas step delicately through the reeds, and yellow weavers build nests that hang heavy on spring-loaded branches. The tranquil camp brings out the tiredness in me after the long days on the bike, and I opt to stay a second night. Also staying are two American researchers who spend their days digging for fossils in the Tugen Hills. Perhaps they will find more remains of our ancestors.

That night, sounds from the endless African bush mimic a too-loud nature soundtrack: squawking, hooting, calling, rustling and stridulation. At three o'clock I get up and record the cacophony that engulfs the *banda*. I am kept awake for most of the two nights that I stay yet, strangely, in the mornings I am more refreshed than if I had slept the nights through.

With some reluctance I leave the camp and ride south, crossing the equator for the sixth time in ten days. I take a photo on a little platform that has been built in front of a huge metal globe to mark the crossing. The district commissioner arrives to plan the finish line celebrations of Sunday's half-marathon, perhaps in preparation for next month's Olympic Games in London. Maybe this would be a good moment to visit Iten, the centre of Kenyan long-distance athletics. The town, perched high on the western escarpment of the Rift Valley, is a few hours' ride away.

At 2,400 metres, the weather towards the Elgeyo Escarpment is cloudy, chilly and damp, and the air is noticeably thin and heady. After riding uphill on a twisty road for what seems like a lifetime, I reach a large square arch over the road that proclaims, "Welcome to Iten. Home of Champions".

I ride the length of the muddy town looking for a likely place to stay. I park up next to a group of teenagers in pristine burgundy jerseys and Prince of Wales check skirts. It's another one of those occasions in Africa when I am troubled by the distance between my shabby appearance and the locals' ability to look effortlessly stylish. With red mud clinging to my boots, I trudge past the Joyland Tea Room: a corrugated shack where, in the doorway, a baby plays alphabet blocks with lumps of charcoal. A man catches my eye.

'I can recommend the Jambo Hotel,' he says. 'It is fine-fine.'

I check out the hotel, but it is less than fine-fine. It's not even fine. It doesn't have a room without a ceiling covered in mould, and I sense a hint of threat, which I later realise is just a mixture of low spirits and indifference.

I return to the street and leave the bike with two men playing bottle-top draughts near the London Marathon store, a leaning shack of indeterminate purpose shaped like a parallelogram. I already feel the lack of oxygen at the altitude; what's worse is that if you're not going downhill in Iten, you're going up, so physical activity is a struggle. Later I learn that Iten has derived its name from 'Hill Ten'. The other nine must be a fright. Which makes the success of this town as a training centre for top athletes all the more remarkable. Or, perhaps, perfectly sensible, because Iten has produced an astonishing number of world-class, long distance runners, and now attracts athletes from around the world who come to push their bodies in the thin air and discover the training secrets of the experts.

Outside the Living Faith Church Worldwide ("Home of Signs, Wonders and Miracles"), three athletes jogging in brightly coloured training gear come to a halt. The skintight leggings, branded, zippered tops and fluorescent running shoes remind me of the other-worldliness of the Samburu people in the desert: 3D in a 2D world. One recommends that I stay at Lornah's place, which sounds cosy enough – but Lornah's place turns out to be the High Altitude Training Centre, home of the elite runners.

'Why would I stay where the athletes train?' I ask.

'You are in Iten,' says a runner in an orange tracksuit. That was an answer, but not to my question.

'You may not realise it, but I'm no athlete,' I say.

'If there is room, maybe Lornah will take you in.'

As much as I love watching athletics on TV, my approach to running is simple: I want to have done it, but I don't want to be doing it. Runner or not, I am already curious to meet the people who can train with so little oxygen.

Off the main road I find a large, well-maintained compound with buildings set around an immaculate swimming pool. Opposite a two-storey building there is a modern block with what looks like a college refectory. There is a languid air about the place, as though someone has turned down the speed of the day. A steady stream of poised and elegant athletes stretch their legs like they're stepping through long grass.

The gym manager, a whippet in a tracksuit called Richard, takes charge of me and says he will find me a room. He asks for more than I have yet paid for accommodation in Kenya, but it includes all meals, and the atmosphere is so relaxed that it promises to be worth the extra. Considering the long ride and the state of the Jambo Hotel, the day seems to have swerved into something better than I could have expected.

Richard brings me to the dining room and tells me to help myself to a buffet-style meal laid out on a counter. Then the assistant manager of the training centre arrives, Willy Songkok, whose name, thankfully, is pronounced *Son-gok*.

I wolf down the nettle soup, organic wild rice, grated cabbage and salad.

The soft-spoken man says, 'Your food is the same as the athletes have eaten. You are lucky that we have room. We are always fully booked for the European winter months, November to April. You just missed Mo Farah and Paula Radcliffe and all the others.'

Then Songkok brings me a soft drink and explains the set-up at the centre.

'We have everything that an athlete needs,' he says. 'The food is controlled and healthy, there is no smoking or alcohol allowed on site. They come here and must concentrate on their training. Nothing else. With distractions they lose their focus. The UK team coaches love sending their athletes here because they know there is nothing else for them to do but train and eat and sleep. There is not even internet or TV in their rooms.'

He laughs. 'But there is one exception: Mo Farah. He says he cannot live without his precious Manchester United, so Lornah extended the TV service to his room. You see the one with the wire? That is his room.'

While we are talking, Songkok is interrupted by a constant stream of calls to his cellphone, and he speaks to every caller with care and gentle politeness.

'Now, you have eaten well? I will show you your room. Paula Radcliffe was staying in this room recently. This very one.'

All the rooms are identical. They have running water, a firm bed with one pillow and a blanket, a tiled bathroom, but not much else. They are too modern and clean to be called spartan, but I'm sure for an international track star the standard is below what they are used to.

We discuss Kenyan success on the track and why so many top runners come from Iten.

Songkok says, 'People come from all over the world to learn from our training styles: the altitude, the food, the routine. It is all equally important. One thing, and only one thing, works in Kenya: running!'

'And physique?' I ask, encouraging him to talk.

'Yes. The runners are mostly from the Kalenjin tribe. We are all Kalenjin. Very tall, very skinny. Sometimes the Kenyans look sick, they are so thin. And if they are not born in Iten, they move here to be near the training centre. How do they run, I wonder? The Kenyan does not know when to stop running. By comparison, Europeans look healthy, too healthy, when they come here. The European listens to his body. When it hurts he slows down. But a Kenyan does not stop, no matter how much it hurts, because he fears he would be thought a coward.'

Perhaps that is their secret.

He says, 'The one man the Kenyans are worried about for the Olympics is Mo Farah. He is *very* powerful. Like the Kenyan, he will not give up. He does not know how!'

We walk around the sparkling pool, and he says, 'It is quiet now because most athletes sleep in the afternoon. Thursday and Tuesday are very big training days. Very heavy. They get up early, then train, then breakfast, then train, then lunch, then sleep, then train again in the afternoon.'

Songkok wheels my bike to a lock-up shed.

'Will you sell it to me? I would like such a bike.'

'Meet me in Nairobi in a few weeks,' I say. 'We'll make a deal.'

He then lends me his laptop so I can update my blog using the wi-fi in the lounge, and gives me his cellphone to call home. He is falling over himself to help me, even though I only arrived an hour ago – I haven't even checked in yet. In fact, I never do check in, and am never asked for money until I am packed and ready to leave after three days.

Later, I meet Victor Kipchirchir Chesang, a nineteen-year-old, 3,000-metre steeplechaser. He must be at least 6' 3", with legs long enough to step over the barriers.

'We have an advantage, it is true,' he says. 'There are many athletes from Iten and we train hard. Doctors believe we are strong because of the haemoglobin in our blood; but we have lived at altitude for many generations, so the Kalenjin are used to thin air. When we race in Europe, we find it so easy to breathe; but if I leave Iten I think my times will not be fast.'

We head towards the lounge where some of the athletes are watching TV. Giraffe-like, Victor seems to move slowly but covers a staggering amount of ground. I'm almost jogging to keep up.

'Many do not get in the Kenyan team,' he says, 'so they run for other countries with a new passport. Some run for Qatar or Bahrain, but do not run their fastest times after they leave this place. The air is special here.'

He is proud to tell me that his best time is 8.31.07, just thirty-eight seconds off the steeplechase world record.

I say, 'I'll look out for you at the Rio Olympics.'

'I will be there,' he says, seriously.

After an afternoon nap (why shouldn't I behave like a champion?), I meet the man from the village who gave me directions to the Jambo Hotel. His name is Hillary.

'You do not like the Jambo?' he says.

'It was grim. Even for me.'

'You have travelled far?'

'Nairobi,' I say, 'via the desert.'

'You must be tired from the ride. And sore.'

'You're not kidding. What do you do here?'

'I am the physio,' says Hillary.

Just the man.

An hour later, in my underpants, I ease myself up onto the massage table in the treatment room. Within two minutes Hillary is pummelling my body with no mercy. Instead of warming up the muscles and working up to the knotty shoulders, neck and legs, he attacks them cold. I can't think what I have said that might have upset him.

'These muscles must be stretched,' he says.

'All at once?'

I am in agony and breathless.

'You will sleep tonight,' he says.

'But will I wake up?' I gasp.

'It is too much?' he asks, not expecting an answer.

He is going at my ribcage with all his weight and trying to force my whole body through the little hole in the bench for my face. I cannot form a single intelligible sound.

'Mo Farah was on this bench last week,' he says.

That makes me feel a *lot* better.

'He did not complain!'

Dinner is a home-made pizza, cabbage, *ugali* (a Kenyan staple made from corn dough), ratatouille and watermelon. Any more of this high-energy food and I'll be joining the next training session. I eat with a young, fair-haired Englishman who is coaching a number of athletes based in the village.

'Most are signed up with a European or American coaching team,' he says. 'They all have agents who arrange their trips abroad to compete in marathons and meets throughout the world. It can provide a good income for them while it lasts.'

'I have noticed that most of the athletes are locals,' I say, 'but all the agents and coaches are white Europeans.'

'That's true. One day it might change. We only offer the last ten per cent, maybe the final five per cent improvement on athletes who are already phenomenally talented. They need help to pace themselves so that they are prepared for each event, otherwise a Kenyan will run and run and train and train with no recovery. This limits their success, shortens their careers and reduces their income.'

We are joined by two Japanese sports journalists who write for a national newspaper in Tokyo. They say that Kenyan athletics is big news in Japan, so even the trials will be reported in depth.

'The Olympic trials are this weekend,' says the coach.

'Who's favourite to get the three places for each event?' I ask.

The journalists move in close to hear the reply.

'It doesn't matter who gets the places,' says the coach. 'I specialise in marathon runners, and the standard is so high that the selectors could pick any three from twelve that we are training. Last year, the top twenty marathon runners in the world were all Kenyan.'

That night I hang out in the lounge with the two Japanese. When they leave to file their stories, I read a newspaper article about Maasai from the *Ilkololik* age set (young *morani*) who have killed six lions about 100 kilometres south of Nairobi. The disturbing photograph of the six carcasses is the front page splash. The Kenya Wildlife Service tried to save the lions after it heard they were cornered by the *morani,* but it was too late to save them. The warriors are quoted as saying that, regardless of the sport involved, if the lions kill their livestock, they are justified in hunting the big cats.

Songkok arrives and sees the front page headline. He has a more sanguine approach to the story.

'Every *moran* should kill at least one lion and take its tail as part of the ritual of reaching manhood,' he says. 'One *moran* from that region has collected seven tails. They hunt with no protection or vehicles and only use spears. Could you kill a lion with only a spear, Alan? I do not have that courage.'

It is chilly in the lounge, so Songkok brings an open brazier of burning coals to warm the room.

'I am glad I can understand your accent,' he says. 'The Welsh. Oh! And the Irish! They speak too fast. But the worst was a man from Stoke: I had to read his lips to know what he was saying! Is it the same language, Alan?'

He loves to make people laugh.

'Have you met Lornah?' he asks. 'You know who she is?'

'Not really.'

'She was world cross-country champion and holds some world records. She has won city marathons all over the world. She married a Dutch, you may see the white man, but still she returned to Iten to start the Lornah Kiplagat Foundation and build this centre.'

I warm myself by the fire.

'Alan, would you like a beer?'

'Can't,' I say. 'I'm in training.'

'As long as you can prove that you are a coach and not an athlete, you are okay!'

'Fair enough.'

'Cold or warm?'

He brings a cold bottle of Tusker, opens it and hands it to me with all the care of a night nurse. I have never met a man so enthusiastic on so little encouragement.

'Songkok,' I say, 'I appreciate your kindness to me since I arrived.'

'Not you only,' he says indifferently.

'So you are this kind to everyone?' I ask.

'So it must be.'

The next morning I ride through wilting cornfields to what locals call 'the stadium': a red-dirt running track consisting of vague lanes marked out with sprinkled chalk around a grassy in-field, with goalposts at either end. I park up next to the top bend. There are a few teams of neon-clad athletes working out on the track, sprinting then jogging, sprinting then jogging in twos and threes. Along the back straight is a string of wooden buildings with decaying tin roofs that look as though they may be inhabited by squatters. Laundry stretched along a washing line flutters within two metres of the outside lane. Further along, acacia trees shade the runners before they reach the final bend, which opens up with vertiginous views down the valley. I stroll over to the wooden stand, a neglected blue structure with twenty rows of bench seating below a roof that should really be condemned. After watching the training for half an hour and walking the outside lane, I become aware of my breathing, which is laboured and raspy. Iten is wearing me out.

I continue around the banked terrace back to my bike and prepare to leave, when one of the runners who has been warming down nearby comes over. She is so thin she could slip through a letterbox.

'You are an agent?' she asks.

'No.'

'A manager? Or coach?'

'Just a fan.'

'This is curious,' she says, 'most white men in Iten work with the athletes.'

I attach the tank bag to the bike and prepare to leave.

'Do you ride to the main road?' she asks. 'I will show you the quick way.'

'Jump on.'

The athlete has no outer tracksuit, so gets on the bike wearing her running gear. As we leave the stadium I see that school is out. A primary schoolteacher leads a class of uniformed six-year-olds up the dirt road, like blue streamers trailing behind a ship. I ride dead slow beside the teacher to chat as most of the children come up to me and shake my hand, which strikes me as an impressively formal gesture for ones so young. Every few metres we lose a child who scrambles through a hedge, or darts into a rough track and runs home. Eventually there are just two children left, who jump into a ditch before scaling a fence and sprinting across a raised field towards a mud hut. They run easier than they walk.

The teacher catches my eye and says, 'Future champions.'

Beatrice, the athlete on the back of the bike, wants to introduce me to her family. We ride to a brick house behind a metal fence near the main road. Tethered livestock ruminate under some washing on a line.

'This is my home,' she says. 'And this is my cow.'

Three excited kids run out of the house. 'And these are my children.'

Inside, her sister, who has been babysitting, brings me a cup of milky tea poured from a flask. T

Even though I am treated to a rich welcome, it is hard not to notice the house is in a poor state. It's hard to tell if the walls are in the process of being repaired or have been left to disintegrate, and there is a hole in the ceiling large enough for a man to crawl through.

Beatrice raises her hand and says, 'These are my medals.'

Decorating the four walls are scores of medals dangling from lanyards won at athletics meets around the world. On every surface sit dusty cups, trophies and presentation shields; the zig-zag burgundy flag of Qatar is unfurled around a dresser.

'We have both won many races,' says Beatrice. 'My husband now runs for Qatar. They came and took five Kenyans to run for their country. He is not a Muslim. He is Kalenjin. They offer him the money, they change his name and now he can help our children. It is for the best.'

'Where is he now?' I ask.

'Running a marathon. In Madrid, I think. Where is that?'

On my second night in Iten I meet Lornah Kiplagat, the founder of the training centre, an elegant woman of around thirty-five years of age. She is wearing a thick pullover and heavy sweatpants, and her hair is in braids pulled tight in the Kalenjin fashion.

'I have come from the treatment room,' she says. 'My daily massage. I feel fresh!'

'With Hillary?' I ask.

'He is wonderful, no?'

'He's all right if you like medieval torture.'

She laughs a laugh of recognition and thanks God for Hillary. She then thanks God for Songkok and all the staff for making the centre what it is and helping the foundation raise money for girls' education.

'In Kenya, if there is little money in the home, only the boy will be educated. I want to build a school and make sure girls have good educations, so that they can return to their villages with knowledge and make a difference. Who knows, they may make a difference with athletics.'

'Where do your athletes come from?' I ask.

'All over Africa, and we look after them all. Especially now that the track at the stadium has improved.'

'Really?' I say, trying not to reveal my true impression.

'Were you there today?' she asks.

'Yes.'

'Were there cows and sheep on the in-field?'

'Not today.'

'I told you!' she says. 'Things are improving! But when we fill the water jump for the steeplechase it attracts the goats and cattle. Other times there is a football match going on in the middle while we are racing around the track.'

'The stand looks as if it won't be standing for much longer,' I say, 'and the shacks on the back straight –'

'They are not shacks! The police live there!'

She laughs easily.

'It is not like this in Europe,' she says. 'I live in the Netherlands and the facilities are good. No cows on the infield. So I thought, why should we not have good facilities in Iten? That is why I built this centre. The track I can do nothing about because the council owns it. That is why I want to build my own stadium. One day we will have an international meeting here for the very best athletes from around the world. Of course, many of them are already here!'

A teenage girl in running gear spots Lornah from across the way. She politely excuses her presence, then curtsies for Lornah. The girl is overcome with gratitude for being allowed to train at the centre, and thanks Lornah half a dozen times.

'Are you training hard?' asks Lornah.

'Yes, thank you,' she says. 'Yes, oh yes. I will not give up. You can be sure of me.'

She bows, then hugs Lornah like a mother. She walks off happy.

Lornah says, 'Have you seen her run? This Ugandan girl is good but will be better with our help. Maybe one day we will have a Ugandan champion.'

Lornah's instinct is not a fanciful prediction. Wilson Kipsang, a local man, would later win the 2012 London marathon more than two minutes ahead of Martin Lel in second place, also from the district. Four of the first ten men across the line were from this province and the first five women were all Kenyan, the initial letter of their family names giving a clue to their Kalenjin roots: Mary Keitany, Edna Kiplagat, Priscah Jeptoo, Florence Kiplagat and Lucy Kabuu. Even though running is so ingrained in the culture, it is still staggering that Kenyans posted twenty-nine of the thirty fastest official marathon times in 2011.

The altitude, genetic make-up and fierce competition for places accounts for some of their astounding results. After a short visit, it seems to me that there is no magic ingredient; or if there is, it takes root in desire – a desire to win by training harder and longer than their competitors. It is lucky for international sport that people are emerging from the impoverished countryside to grab a chance to run in professional meetings abroad. In this sense, sport becomes an instrument to solve a bigger problem and take people from a shack to a breeze-block house, from village schooling for their children to college education, from Rift Valley isolation to international fame. Sometimes a desire to escape from poverty can be the greatest motivator – and not only for their own generation. How many dreams are created in the minds of children each time an athlete returns to the village with a medal or trophy, or a winner's cheque from Boston, Berlin or Sydney?

Teenagers must see cousins and uncles living in relative luxury and compare it to their own lives shortly destined for hand-to-mouth farming or low-paid work, and decide to put in the hours of training to emulate their heroes. Which is why tomorrow morning, Beatrice will join the hundreds of brightly attired athletes weaving and bobbing like clockwork toys over the dirt roads and paths that carve through the town. Future champions.

Next day I see Hillary and Richard, the gym manager, on my way to breakfast.

'How do you feel?' asks Hillary.

'Loose,' I say. 'It feels like my limbs don't belong to me anymore.'

He slaps my palm.

'But,' I add, 'I had the best night's sleep of my whole trip.'

'I told you. And you are before me now, so you did wake up!'

Richard says, 'You must come to the gym and stretch the muscles that Hillary worked on. You will feel better. There are not many athletes in today. You may come.'

I'm not totally convinced that I need a gym workout, but I can see that Richard is keen to be useful on a slow day and I don't want to disappoint him. Even though I only have street clothes, I walk over to the gym. It's a walk I shouldn't have taken.

Next to the sleek and honed Richard, I feel – and look, in the brutally revealing floor-to-ceiling mirrors – like an uncoordinated child in a romper room, in my socks and cargo trousers. He takes me around every machine in the gym, and encourages me to attempt weights I last lifted twenty years ago: quads then chest and triceps, back and biceps, shoulders, hamstrings and calves.

'I think my body may have had enough,' I say after five machines.

'It is okay,' he says.

'Thanks. I'll get some breakfast.'

'No,' says Richard. 'I mean it is okay to continue. Keep going. You are getting stronger – and younger! I like it.'

I couldn't agree less, but keep going as best I can and skip reps whenever he's not watching. He keeps pushing me and finds ever more devious uses for the machines that now resemble devices from a dungeon. He then lays out a mat and gets me to curl and stretch into positions my body hasn't experienced for a decade. I'm dying. Eventually the decision to quit is taken away from both of us when I crumple in the middle of one repetition and he sends someone for water.

My other torturer, Hillary, comes in and asks, 'What happened to you? Are you sick? Do you need more work in the treatment room?'

I find a quiet corner of the changing room, curl up and expect my heart to burst at any moment. A streamlined, naked athlete who looks carved from ebony and therefore couldn't look any less like how I feel, steps out of the shower and throws me a towel. I drape it over my head and wait for him to leave before I come out and face the world.

6

OUT WEST

After two nights in Iten, and with every muscle in my body cramping, quivering or begging for mercy, I head out of the mountains towards the small Western Province that hugs the eastern shore of Lake Victoria. It is a relatively impoverished region yet seems richly fertile, with sweeping cornfields where ragged children pull at five-metre lengths of sugar cane from the backs of slow-moving tractors heading for the refinery. Luo *dalas,* or homesteads, dot the landscape, the number of huts inside each compound indicating the number of wives within. The landscape and the threatening weather fill me with melancholy, but things could be worse. I brighten a little when I come across a little workshop of coffin makers called "Golden Dreams".

I stop for the night in the provincial capital, Kakamega, and step through the rain into my hotel's lean-to bar to work up an appetite for the curry house next door. There are two middle-aged women sitting at a table, and an older man on his own with two half-drunk bottles of beer in front of him.

The man is very merry and having a cheerful conversation with nobody in particular, enough for me to infer that he has been here a while. He catches my eye. After ten minutes trying to have a detached conversation from opposite ends of the bar, Wycliffe, for that is his name, invites me to join him. He orders four more bottles of beer – two each.

I tell him about my time with the athletes in Iten, and how impressed I was by their dedication to their sport.

Wycliffe, round-shouldered and fat-fingered, says, 'They are Kalenjin type. They are tall and skinny. Of course they run, to keep warm! We are Luhya type. I will tell you precisely where the Luhya are. We are here! Around the lake.'

The bar drinkers, plate-faced and wide-eyed, look very different to the taut-skinned people in the mountains.

'We are forty-two tribes in Kenya,' says Wycliffe. 'United by precisely two things only: English and Swahili, the language from the coast.'

His speech, dipping and swooping and loose, is like improvisational jazz. I can't always catch the tune of it, but I know the conversation is practically singing.

He engages with one of the two women who are about to leave. She sits down with her handbag on her lap. He may be slurring his words, but his questions are forensically direct: What is your name? What is your job? Where do you live? Why have you come to this bar on this night? Once she has answered to his satisfaction, she asks him for his cellphone number and, with a killer flash of her enormous eyes, says that she 'will be around later'.

After she leaves, Wycliffe takes on the look of a man about to perform in a play, searching for an audience, preparing his stage marks. He takes a big breath.

'I will tell you precisely, Alan,' he says, trying out my name. 'The world has changed. How the world has changed, Alan. Before, the man would chase the woman. Now, the woman chases the man. Yet I cannot fault it!'

Although he is wearing a creased leather jacket and has the dishevelled look of a market trader, it turns out that Wycliffe is headteacher of a boarding school a few kilometres out of town. He writes down the name and address of the school and makes me promise that I will come and address morning assembly at some unspecified point in the future.

'What should I talk about?'

'Inspire them!' he says, appalled that I should need to ask.

We slurp our beer. There is a sleepy air in the bar and the waitresses are bored and listless. I hear the thickening of an oncoming crowd, before the atmosphere catches its breath when a large group of men walk in through the bead-curtain of rain that now pours from the plastic roof. Most of the men seem on edge as they make a close inspection of everybody in the bar. Taking up the rear is a stylishly dressed man in chinos and a yellow and black shirt with the letters UDF printed on the sleeves. The bar is now full, and the new arrivals are the only issue in the place.

The man in yellow and black greets everyone with a mixture of solicitude and condescension, wheedling, it seems to me, just enough information to confirm a private prejudice. He shakes hands, including those of the bar staff, but neither Wycliffe's nor mine. I begin to feel as though I'm at a private party without an invitation.

'Did you notice that he did not shake my hand?' says Wycliffe. 'Even though it is so important in Africa to touch flesh. He does not want to be seen associating with me. Nor my new friend.'

'Why?' I ask, thinking it might be because he has had too much to drink.

'I will tell you precisely, Alan. Because he is the MP for this region: Dr Bonny Khalwale, if you please.'

Two minders standing close by pick up on our conversation and glare at Wycliffe.

'So?' I ask.

'So. I may be his opposition in the next election, this December,' he says, as if addressing a crowd. 'He is local, as am I. We went to the same school, so he is no better than I.'

All the minders, security and hangers-on shoot Wycliffe dagger looks. Khalwale glances over dismissively. I keep my eyes firmly on Wycliffe's and lower my voice in the hope that he will follow my lead.

'I see,' I say, 'and UDF means...?'

'United *Democratic* Forum,' says Wycliffe in a voice dripping with incredulity. 'It is a new party to fight the election. He has left the New Ford Kenya party.'

I am not sure that I have heard him correct, so ask him to repeat it. He gets louder.

'Precisely speaking: the New Forum for the Restoration of Democracy in Kenya. "New Ford" for short.'

The waitresses look on, waiting for direction from the group of men who now run the bar. Eventually the entourage push three tables together and sit down. A minder, like a well-trained butler anticipating his master's needs, steals cushions from other seats and places two for the back and three for the seat, before the MP places his behind on the prepared chair directly in front of the TV set high on a wall. Although most of the entourage are creepily deferential to the MP, an old man wearing a loud UDF shirt seems unaware of the fuss – mostly because he is monumentally drunk. Wycliffe is now not the most inebriated man in the bar.

Everybody else's eyes are on Khalwale. He wants a cigarette, the others fight to be the first with a match. He calls for a drink, then everybody orders one for themselves. He tells a story and everybody in the entourage laughs in the appropriate pauses. He confers seriously and they all adopt worried brows. The MP scans the bar once more, as though looking for assassins, and everyone copies him.

Wycliffe is still ordering beers in fours and I find myself drinking more than I'd planned; but no matter how much I drink, the strange activity in the bar keeps me sober. Then a young woman arrives, and Khalwale orders a minion at the end of the table to vacate his seat so that she can sit down. The unfortunate man takes a seat at another table in the second division of hangers-on. From that point the man acts as seat-warmer for anyone who vacates a spot near his boss. Perhaps they are concerned he will get lonely, or that he might be perceived by other drinkers as friendless.

Then Khalwale invites the girl to an empty table for a private word.

'A girlfriend,' says Wycliffe, within earshot of all. 'He can attract them now he is an MP.'

A minder nods at Wycliffe, storing the insult like a promise.

Sitting shoulder-to-shoulder with the girl, Khalwale has the demeanour of a priest listening to a heartfelt confession, but my guess is they are arranging to meet later this evening.

Fascinating though it is to an outsider, Khalwale, Wycliffe, the entourage and the silenced waitresses create a stiff atmosphere in the bar that needs draining. Then Khalwale's image appears on the TV news. He orders everybody in the bar to be silent, and turns up the volume from the remote control. On the screen, wearing the same yellow and black shirt, he is interviewed in Swahili before footage is shown of him speaking at a rally in English.

As soon as the news segment is finished, without forewarning, Khalwale leaves the bar and gets into a thrumming 4x4. Everyone else downs their drinks and steps after him through the rain. One bullish minder stops at our table and whispers something in Wycliffe's ear, but he shrugs it off like an old warrior. He refuses to tell me what was said, but I take it to be more threatening than just political rivalry. The entourage forget to bring along the drunk man whose face is in collapse and who is now swaying in his chair, trying to focus on the television. Fifteen minutes later, when he realises he has been dumped, he staggers off into the waterlogged night.

Next morning I return to the curry restaurant where I was tempted in last night by an overly keen waiter: 'Look, other *mzungus* eat here!' I then went to my room with a notice pinned to the door that read, "Leave your shoes outside your room between 7 p.m. and 9 p.m. for vanishing". I spent a strange night punctuated by the snoring of a man who was going for some sort of record, an ardent couple in the next room who were bound to win a prize, and a car alarm that surely must have been plugged into the mains. After an hour – *at 3 a.m.* – a girl from reception decided to find the owner of the wailing vehicle by knocking on every single door in the hotel and shouting, 'Is it you? Subaru?'

Before I left Britain I promised a friend that I would visit the site of a proposed nursery school for which she was raising money. Jennifer Jaynes's email said that the project was in a place called Irovo, "on the edge of Kakamega where the Yala River comes out of the forest", and that I should "ask for Pastor Jotham Keseko".

Those directions sound perfectly adequate for someone looking for a village in the English countryside, but in the Western Province of Kenya it is like searching for an overweight Kalenjin.

Over breakfast I meet a fellow guest who tries to help me locate Irovo; difficult, not least because two waiters tell me that there is no letter 'v' in Swahili. After four phone calls, the fellow guest is convinced that he has tracked it down and gives me directions towards Lake Victoria.

'It is one and a half hours,' he says. 'You will be swiftly there.'

Following a morning of roadside directions that contradict the man in the restaurant, I find Irovo (Irobo) at the bottom of a steep, muddy track. It is Sunday, and I ride past locals making their way up the hill to the Catholic church. They are dressed as if going to a cabaret at the Talk of the Town: frilly shirts, rainbow-coloured combinations, shimmery tops and formal satin dresses. Unfortunately they must hold up their long skirt hems and trouser turn-ups to keep out of the wash of mud that sloshes over their ankles. This morning I am contributing to it.

Despite the wet conditions underfoot, the heat of the sun is building, so everyone's top half is crisply dry to compensate for the soggy bottom. I find a group of ragged-trousered youths watching the clouds from prone positions on the side of a mud bank. Clearly not Catholics.

'Irovo?' I shout.

'You have found it,' says the eldest.

'Is Pastor Jotham Keseko here?' I ask.

'He is coming.'

I ride the bike up onto the bank, in front of a sweep of mud-and-wattle buildings laid out in an L-shape that look as if they won't last the week. One good storm could see them off. Forty minutes later a man wearing a peach-coloured shirt, pin-striped trousers and a well-knotted tie arrives. He is carrying an infant. The man has a smile that illuminates the compound; his eyes shine.

'Pastor Jotham Keseko?'

'No. I am sorry, I am not the man you seek,' he says. 'I am Pastor Vitalis Tivis Matalo.'

'I'm looking for a place called Irovo,' I say.

'*This* place is called Irovo,' he says.

'I'm looking for a pastor who is trying to build a school.'

'*I* am trying to build a school.'

'Pastor Jotham is building a nursery.'

'*I* am building a nursery.'

He nods at one of the mud brick buildings as the baby gurgles in his arms.

'There are many Irovos,' he says.

I seem to have wasted the morning searching for the wrong Irovo. Even if that is so, I am quickly warming to Pastor Vitalis, and know that this Irovo is probably as good as the next one.

'I made a mistake,' I say. 'This *is* the Irovo I was looking for.'

'But you did not know it until you reached it!' he says.

Which sounds like the wisest utterance I've ever heard, especially after the night with Wycliffe and the rival MP.

Vitalis slaps my hand and lights up the compound once more. This is his cue to give me the grand tour. He unlocks the padlock on a home-made door, and takes me into an unlit room with tipsy walls and a few benches that could double as both desks and pews. There is a truck tyre on the floor, perhaps used as a seat for a little one. A teacher has written lessons directly onto cut-up maize sacks which are hung on the walls. They show the alphabet, vowel sounds, numbers and shapes. The blackboard is so inadequate that a teacher has continued writing in chalk on the dried mud wall. It is dark because the spaces for windows are boarded up with makeshift shutters; the only light comes from the gaps between the walls and the tin roof.

When I exit the classroom I hear the unmistakable chants of a preacher. Another bare room in the compound has been unlocked since I entered the classroom. Inside, Vitalis' wife is working herself into a frenzy; her rhythmic chants sound like incantations from a mountain top. I pop my head inside, but there are only four other people in the make-do church: a vacant-looking teenager sitting on a bench; a woman standing with her face no more than fifteen centimetres from the back wall; and two children, one of about five years and a baby on the floor clothed in an immaculate white dress.

Vitalis takes me to what he calls his office, another uninviting space without electricity and only a few handmade sticks of furniture to make it useful. In the corner is a stack of firewood. Even though the whole place is beyond bleak, the atmosphere is one of hope and Vitalis is full of precise courtesy. The room may be bare but it is crowded with his dreams. He has big – no, make that prodigious – plans to bring educational and spiritual upliftment to this neighbourhood.

'These people need a church and a school, it is true. It is for me to furnish such things, but the situation, economically speaking, is not the best, yes.'

He is a master of understatement, and constructs his sentences like he has never spoken an unnecessary word in his life.

I say, 'I've travelled in Kenya for a few weeks and it seems to me that the Western region is one of the poorest.'

'We are only poor because of idleness, yesss,' he says. 'If the people have some skills and a purpose and do not follow the curses of idleness and alcohol, we should have no poverty, yesss.'

'How much do the parents pay for the schooling?'

Thoughts are collected from far away before an answer is offered.

'I... *ask them to pay* 1,300 shillings [about £10] after three months – but they only pay it with a lot of difficulty.' He hides his frustration with a laugh. 'Some pay, but others pay only halfway or quarterway. If you are not somewhat patient, you can end up with no school. But I have the heart to raise the project. I have endurance and hope that it will bring a good thing. That will be enough. Maybe tomorrow.'

'Tomorrow' is a very naked-sounding word here, used to mean anytime after the present; yet his enthusiasm is deep and sincere.

'And the teachers?' I ask.

'I pay the teachers 2,500 [about £20] a month. The rent is 4,500 per month. Where I can, I save money. The toilets I made myself, I will be pleased to show you – and I finished these walls and these buildings, yesss. You have to work if you want a good thing. You don't just get it on a silver plate!'

His plate is tin, and he can't escape the arithmetic.

Then we are interrupted by the landlord, a stocky, middle-aged man with a week's stubble who is dressed in old trousers, a woolly hat and a formal shirt that used to be white. Introductions are made. His hand feels like old leather.

Vitalis is newly deferential, and says to me, 'Excuse me, sir. This is an important man.'

They exchange some words before the landlord leaves. I have a feeling that the presence of a white and the possibility of patronage may result in the rent going up.

Past the latrine that he dug himself, Vitalis walks me over to a kiosk-shop with a grill on the counter through which items are passed. He invites me to share a soft drink and buys two tiny packets of biscuits.

'For such a visitor I should kill a cock, but I have not,' he says. 'So I must offer you something.'

He hands me the biscuits and an orange Fanta. Then he picks up a tin cup from the ground into which he pours a little Fanta and allows the baby, wedged between his legs, to sup from it. She suckles the metal lip as if it were her mother, while never taking her eyes off me. As the liquid goes in one end it leaks out the other, and they're both soon sitting in a pool of her wee.

When Vitalis notices, he smiles apologetically and says, 'With you sitting here, she was too frightened to ask.'

He picks her up and the wet dribbles off the bench next to me. He walks her away a few paces, but there is little he can do so he returns to the bench, wipes off the wet with his hand, and replaces her on his knee.

Back at the schoolroom, even though it's Sunday morning, two teachers show up with a small class of kids who are all curious to meet the visitor. Without trying too hard, Vitalis commands the quiet respect of those around him; which is as it should be, because he has a formidable task ahead of him if he wants to turn this collection of tumbledown buildings into a school and church. But he believes that something will turn up and, as he repeats many times, he has hope. For me, it is another example of how sometimes Africa and Africans can survive on a diet of myth. As James Joyce wrote: *The beautiful ineffectual dreamer who comes to grief against hard facts.* Perhaps this predicament is the essence of faith when everything else seems to have given up on you.

Vitalis says, 'I always have hope. A dark room may be lit by a small candle.'

'Or set the world on fire!'

'If it catches.'

He is just the man to light the candle.

It is time for me to go, so I get on the bike.

'God will guide you, wherever you may go,' he says.

It's another difficult leaving, but I am certain the village is in good hands. During our time together Vitalis has crackled with all the promise of a new US$50 bill. So that is exactly what I hand him.

7

MAMA SARAH

Later that same day, in a hotel a few hours' south of Vitalis' embryonic school, Malachi bangs on my door and shouts, 'Mama Sarah will see you. I must take you now. Raise yourself!'

I stir on the mattress, fully clothed, boots and all. I swing my legs off the bed and step outside into the blistering heat. Malachi, a multi-purpose employee from the hotel, leads as we walk single file along a dirt track through healthy cornfields, past trees heavy with ripe bananas. His colleague, Rachel, who was recently taken on at the hotel, walks behind me.

'My name is unusual is it not, my friend?' asks Malachi.

'Malachi is common enough in Ireland.'

'Is it so? It is taken from the Bible. They must be religious in Ireland.'

'Some of them.'

With pride, Rachel says, 'Rachel also is from the Bible.'

We reach a fenced compound of about two acres. The policeman sitting under a tree at the gate puts down his hand of playing cards, leaves his playing partner and asks us to sign in. The visitors' book shows the names of people from a handful of countries, predominantly the USA, who have visited over the last few weeks.

Malachi, Rachel and I then walk up to a modest house with a red tin roof, in front of which is a row of white plastic chairs. Rabbits hop under our feet, turkeys step through the tall grass and sheep graze on anything they can reach. Off to the left are two gravestones.

A young woman invites us to sit. 'Mama Sarah will come,' she says.

Before the front door is opened I notice a sticker on its window: OBAMA '08. Soon, an old woman with stiff joints comes out of the house and steps onto the patch of cut lawn. She has deep lines in her burnt coffee-coloured face, and wears what I take to be a well-practised expression of distrustful curiosity. Mama Sarah is a Luo, the third largest tribe in Kenya, traditionally farmers and fisherfolk. She is wearing a red and pink flowery two-piece outfit and matching headscarf, a pink plastic necklace, bracelets on both wrists and an anklet. On her feet are flip flops, and she holds a wrap over one shoulder. It can't be for the cold. I'm melting.

'Good afternoon, Mama,' I say.

She does not reply. She sits. I sit opposite, two metres away. She begins a conversation with Malachi as she offers her hand to each of us in turn. I have not been in Kenya long enough to distinguish whether they are speaking Swahili or the tribal Dholuo language. I am then invited to ask questions.

'Ask what you wish,' says the young girl, acting as interpreter.

It feels a bit like having an audience with the Pope, except that it's with a faintly distant and crotchety grandmother who mostly refuses eye contact.

Now is a good time to hand over my gifts: two kilograms of flour, one kilogram of sugar and a bottle of cooking oil. The collection of shopping sounds rather prosaic, but they were the most exotic items available in the tiny kiosk shop in the village.

Mama Sarah creases her eyes shut and shows me her spaced, broken teeth in the first smile directed at me.

A translation comes back. 'She will look forward to making a cake with your gifts.'

'Thank you for meeting me,' I say.

'From where have you come?' asks the interpreter.

'I have ridden from Nairobi. But I live near Manchester in England.'

Mama Sarah shakes her head a little at the translation.

'Mama Sarah says that she has never heard of Manchester, but a man visited once from England.'

I want to ask so many questions, but it is not the old woman I am most interested in – it is her grandson.

'Does your grandson write to you? And if he does, what does he say?' I ask.

The translation comes back. 'He is very busy, so I hear from him only occasionally. I cannot read or speak English, so the messages come through other people.'

'How has your grandson's success changed your life?'

I detect a look of incredulity.

'Not at all. I was Mama Sarah before, and I am still Mama Sarah. Only now I am older. Ninety!'

I give her a second to enjoy the moment.

'How do the other villagers treat you?' I ask.

'The same. And why not?'

She is getting testy, so I ditch the pushy questions and try another tack.

'You must be the proudest grandmother in Kenya,' I say.

She grips her wrist and pushes both hands under her bosom as if settling in for an argument.

'Barack Obama is *not* my *only* grandchild!'

The interpreter stands up, which suggests the interview is over.

When I ask if I can take a photo, her assistant brings an envelope for me to make a donation to the village school. I slip in 1,000 Kenyan shillings (about £8). Mama Sarah lightens up and makes small talk with Rachel and Malachi as photographs are taken. She then asks her assistant to fill a plastic bag with mangoes, which are maturing on trees that surround the house. They are collected and handed to Malachi.

My meeting with the grandmother of the world's most powerful man is over. I step away a few paces to the two graves near the edge of the garden. One, covered in chipped and discoloured tiles, is the grave of Mama Sarah's late husband, which shows he died aged 105. Only I seem to think this is remarkable in a country where life expectancy is sixty-three years. The other grave is the last resting place of Barack Obama's namesake father who, as a student on scholarship, met fellow undergraduate Ann Dunham in 1960 at the University of Hawaii. They married the following year and produced their only child, Barack Obama, Jr. The parents of the future President of the United States divorced in 1964, after which Obama, Sr. returned to Kenya. He remarried, but died in a road accident in Nairobi in 1982.

Malachi, Rachel and I walk back to the hotel on the main dirt road through Nyang'oma Kogelo, then down Mama Sarah Obama Road and past Senator Obama Secondary School. We scuff our way back, reluctant to pick up our feet, an effort in this heat.

'Kogelo is a remote place to build such a big hotel,' I say.

'You are correct,' says Malachi. 'A rich man, a Luo, met Obama when he was senator and visited our village. The man built the hotel because of all the tourists that should come when Obama is made president. He won the election, but the crowds did not come.'

Later, with a new closeness between us, as though we have both witnessed the same apparition, I sit in the shade of the hotel awning while Rachel peels two mangoes. The only sound comes from the ever-present cicadas. Inside the door I am watched by the blinking eyes of a fairground-style picture of Obama, Jr. Nothing stirs. The air just above the earth shimmers.

Rewards for travelling to remote parts sometimes come in strange and disparate forms. I was aware that Mama Sarah lived in these parts, but never thought I'd meet her. I expected this episode to be about how I *nearly* met the leader of the free world's grandmother. What I found was a woman so secure in her dotage that she can refer to Mr President as just another grandchild.

'Is Barack from the Bible?' Rachel asks.

'I don't think so,' I say.

'But he is still a good man, no?'

'Oh, yes,' I say, looking up at the winking picture. 'A good man.'

She hands me one of the dripping, peeled mangoes and buries her marble-white teeth into the other.

'Delicious!' she says.

8

THE VICTORIA NILE

I ride west towards Kisumu to pick up the road to the Uganda frontier. As I reach the crest of a low hill I see for the first time the hub of my journey: Lake Victoria. It defines the new horizon. Like a locomotive from the Nairobi Railway Museum, I have slowly chugged my way to the interior. I feel further from Europe with each passing day, uncoupling carriages as I go. Is this how Victorian explorers felt? Probably not. But looking towards the lake, I am touched by something deep: a distinct whiff of the spirit of adventure.

Devon-born John Hanning Speke was the first European to set eyes on the lake in 1858, and named it for the reigning British monarch. The expedition that brought him here was led by the acclaimed explorer Sir Richard Burton, but as the two men got closer to their goal, Burton contracted malaria in Kazeh (now called Tabora, in modern-day Tanzania), a watering place on the slave route to the interior. Frustrated that he could not travel, Burton watched as Speke set forth on 9 July with a small detachment of porters and guides. A few weeks later he reached the lake at Mwanza on the southern shore.

However, the greater prize – one that puzzled European explorers for decades, and became a Victorian obsession – was the discovery of the source of the River Nile. With few scientific instruments at his disposal, Speke made an educated guess that the newly discovered lake was indeed the source of the mighty river. He was correct.

He later wrote, 'I no longer felt any doubt that the lake at my feet gave birth to that interesting river, the source of which has been the subject of so much speculation, and the object of so many explorers.'

On their return to Britain, perhaps piqued that he was absent from the historic discovery, Burton publicly disputed Speke's claim that he had positively identified the source. Other geographers and explorers rallied behind one camp or the other. Later, the explorer and missionary David Livingstone tried and failed to confirm Speke's supposition.

Speke returned to Lake Victoria four years later and, on 28 July 1862, set eyes on an outflow on the northern shore in modern-day Uganda – what came to be known as the Ripon Falls: the mouth of the river that flowed into the Nile.

The case was finally settled thirteen years later by the Welsh-American reporter Henry Morton Stanley (he of "Dr Livingstone, I presume" fame), who came to Africa to find the 'lost' doctor. Stanley circumnavigated the lake in 1875, which both proved that it was a single expanse of water and confirmed that the river that left the Ripon Falls was the only major outlet.

For historical accuracy, it's worth noting that the presence of the lake was already known in North Africa. Twelfth century Muslim geographer and cartographer Muhammad Al Idrisi charted the lake in what would become known as the Al Idrisi map, which dates from the 1160s. The map clearly shows the lake and suggests that it is the source of the Nile – a fact that Europeans only confirmed 700 years later.

Earlier still, an explorer and merchant named Diogenes in first-century Greece reported that he had found the source of the Nile. He claimed that the river flowed from a mountain range that local people called 'the Mountains of the Moon', because of their snowcapped peaks. These reports were accepted by his contemporary Ptolemy, the Greek astronomer and geographer, who included the details in early maps. Today, the evocative term is used to cover the snow-peaked Rwenzori Mountains on the Uganda–Democratic Republic of the Congo border.

I lose sight of the lake as I head north. It is getting hot: so hot that the road surface has melted and buckled into huge ruts caused by trucks pounding the road to the border. I pass house-sized stacks of bricks with smoke issuing from the tops, which turn out to be make-do kilns used for family-run brickworks. The freshly formed bricks are stacked in such a way that leaves a central space in which an open fire burns, drying and firing the bricks in one procedure.

At the Busia border post I allow myself to be taken up by a man in flapping-soled shoes who calls himself a 'clearing agent'. He directs me to immigration where I am relieved of

US$50, then to a container where I am sold Ugandan bike insurance for US$85. Then there's a hiccup. He darts in and out of an office that I assume must be Kenyan customs. He says that the officer needs to verify the make and model of the bike, but it does not show on her computer screen.

'You must leave the original purchase document with her,' he says, 'and pick it up on your return through Busia.'

Then I drop the bombshell.

'I'm not returning through Busia. I'm going on to Rwanda and around the lake.'

He flaps off to the office to impart the news. He returns very vexed.

'I must have 2,500 shillings. You must come! But you must say you only go to Uganda and return to Busia.'

'No, I'm going further,' I say.

'I know!' he says. 'But you must not tell her! Whatever she says, you must say that you will return! Your bike has no papers. She will quiz you.'

I step into the little office. A plump woman in uniform, who looks as if she's grown up in the space between her chair and the desk, has my passport, Ugandan immigration and insurance documents under an elbow. I force a smile and offer my hand, but she just looks at me over the top of her glasses without moving her head. I have misjudged the mood, and quickly retract it.

'This bike is not on my computer,' she says. 'How is it so?'

'New model,' I say. 'That's computers.'

She doesn't smile. She talks as if she is holding me away from her by my tail.

'Registration?'

'It's brand new,' I say. 'I didn't have time to register the bike.'

She is getting exasperated with me.

'You tell me it is not registered for Kenya... and you want to travel to other nations! Where you go?'

'Kampala.'

'You go to Rwanda?' she asks.

I sense the minder shifting uneasily behind me. She is willing him to intervene so she can tear up the papers, I have no doubt.

'No,' I say. 'Just Uganda.'

'You go to Tanzania?'

'Heavens, no.'

'Burundi?'

'No way.'

She looks the look that makes me feel like a nine-year-old caught lying. She glances at the clearing agent.

'We have to discuss the matter,' she says. 'I will write a manual form. It is not normal.'

'Okay,' says the minder. 'Now you go.' He pushes me towards the door.

I gather a little dignity and head back out into the blazing sun. A little while later the minder exits the office with a form that he says should allow me to travel. He has not seen such a form before and tries to reckon what he has been given. By some strange coincidence the form has space for entry and exit through five borders, enough for Uganda, Rwanda, Burundi, Tanzania and back to Kenya.

'By chance the woman has given you your journey, *mzungu.*'

Holding my papers aloft, he leads me and the bike through the throng to the swing gate – my entrance into Uganda.

'Now you pay two thousand,' he says.

'I just gave you twenty-five hundred!'

'That was for the paperwork.'

'What?'

'The officer! The woman in uniform.' He rustles his fingers. 'It had to be done.'

On the other side of the barrier (appropriately, considering the 'border-to-border' origin of their epithet), dozens of boda-boda riders, wearing identical uniforms of pink shirts and grey trousers, stand beside their bicycles fitted with passenger cushions arranged over the back wheel. What a brilliant way to enter a new country.

The road towards Jinja is flat and straight. I pass cornfields and rice paddies and am imbued with the feeling I've achieved something today. Then the bike jumps out of gear on a colossal speed bump and the chain comes off the sprocket. Either by chance or arrangement there is a motor workshop five metres away. Almost before I realise what has happened, someone with a spanner in hand is replacing the chain.

Even by African standards, there are a conspicuous number of people carrying guns in Uganda. They are so common that they are often held with an insouciance not worthy of their potential. As I prepare to leave the roadside workshop, I see a boy of no more than fifteen swinging a rifle like a cricket bat as he walks barefoot among the shacks.

That night, in Jinja, a hotel receptionist convinces me to stay because she promises to do my laundry immediately and, 'We have multi-channel satellite'. That would make a nice change – but what she neglects to tell me is that the televisions in all the rooms are connected to her screen in reception, so every time she changes channels, so do ours. I think she might have attention-deficit disorder, because the screen does not remain on any one programme for more than two minutes all evening.

Despite President Idi Amin having expelled most Indians from Uganda in 1972, there are many Indian restaurants and clothing stores on Jinja's dusty streets, alongside African women wearing traditional *gomas* (billowy, full-length dresses with short sleeves and pointed tufts on the shoulders).

The bike's worsening mechanical problems eventually catch up with me; bad news generally does. So next morning I find an oily man with a spanner who quickly diagnoses the problem as a faulty power pack. After swapping my new one for a tatty replacement taken from a write-off leaning against a wall, which does not solve the problem, then removing the coil and immediately replacing it because 'I do not have a new one!', I give up and go for some of Uganda's famous coffee.

I share my bike troubles with a man at the café who arranges for a friend to come over. The man is Kenyan and, if nothing else, speaks excellent English, so at least I can explain the symptoms.

'It's like the bike has a stutter with infrequent moments of lucidity,' I say.

'I know the problem!' he says.

He sits on the bike ready to take it for a spin, to check the problem for himself.

'Come right back,' I say, 'and don't do anything until we agree a price!'

He then leaves me in the café. The man's friend at the next table reassures me that he will soon return. He repeats it so many times that I think he is trying to convince himself as much as me. Then he says he has to go, and my heart sinks. Thoughts swirl round my head; not all good ones. Ninety minutes later the mechanic returns.

'Nice bike!' he says.

'Where've you been? Back to Kenya?'

'Now it runs smooth.'

'You've fixed it?' I ask.

'Of course. Stutter means carb.'

Not only has he repaired the machine, but he charges me half my best estimate. On the bike that now feels like I've traded in a Morris Minor for a Bentley, I ride down to the lake shore. On the bank is a memorial to Mahatma Gandhi, some of whose ashes were scattered at this spot. I lean on the pedestal and watch cormorants dive for fish then dry themselves on a branch, a pied kingfisher waiting to breach the surface, a stork balancing in a tree and a bevy of vultures discussing the day's scavenge. Four-foot monitor lizards sun themselves in the shade. It is a scene worthy of the two weeks it has taken me to get here.

A fisherman rows out into the lake and, almost imperceptibly, the boat catches an eddy and turns to face north towards the river mouth known at this point as the Victoria Nile. The boat is soon drifting downstream towards Khartoum a few thousand kilometres away, where the river merges with the Blue Nile. In three months these waters will be in Cairo. This is the spot, on 21 July 1862, where Speke confirmed the source of the White Nile, at that time marked by a cascade he called Ripon Falls. However, because of a dam built downriver in the 1950s, the falls are now submerged below the new water level.

There is a small metal sign: "Source of R. Nile. World's longest river", which seems scant celebration, considering the lengths to which Victorian explorers stretched themselves to find it.

On the other side of the river I find fishermen bailing out leaky boats before pushing off into the swell, spreading their nets on the water's surface and allowing themselves to be taken downstream. Others dry out their clothes on the riverbank. Under the ugly Speke memorial obelisk I am surrounded by vervet monkeys gambolling in the trees. I walk up onto a rise and look north. Despite the source of the Nile being known for over a hundred years, the route to the Mediterranean Sea was only fully navigated for the first time in 2004. Perhaps a future journey beckons.

On the recommendation of a rag-trade Indian in a clothing store, I find a decent curry house. At the door, I wake a slumbering armed man in a too-big uniform who says he will guard my bike while I eat. Before I have entered the doorway, the man curls up with his rifle as though he is bedding down with an old lover.

Later, I walk down the main street into a fringe world of chickens in cages and sofas on the pavement, then stop in the doorway of the first bar that has a seat. For half an hour my drinking companions offer glimpses into their lives that leave me wishing I could drop anchor. They leave when they hear complaining sounds from the treetops that predict the first sign of lightning. There is a lull and then the wind gets up. I move inside at the very moment the heavens open.

There are two barmen, one of whom is playing DJ on a mixer desk. He has headphones and meticulously cues up each track while ignoring requests for drinks. Apart from three youths in the corner, there is only me there. The only stool (which I occupy) is placed in front of a speaker the size of a wardrobe, but the guys in the bar are glued to the TV image above my head: a replay of Andy Murray in a Wimbledon first-round match. Despite the lack of action in the bar area, the dining room out back is packed, where the smells of food do battle with those of the adjacent toilet with no door. The toilet is winning. The wired ambience, the darkness, the blaring sound of rap music, the jolly barmen and Andy Murray's gloomy visage make for an atmosphere that could hardly be more strange. At least that is true before a man who has been fiddling with my bike outside gets the radio working, and calls people out to dance in the rain.

When the bar loses all electricity – on match point! – I brave the downpour, and ride off on the bike-cum-dance machine through muddy puddles and return to where my evening started: the TV of a thousand random channels.

The road through the forest to the capital Kampala (a word derived from 'Impala', a medium-sized antelope) is less than 100 kilometres.

In the city of one and a half million people that feels like triple that, I get a glimpse of Uganda's civility when I go for another bracing curry. It is too much trouble to take the bike down to the street (unbelievably, I have had to ride it up three floors to reach the hotel reception), so I hail a boda-boda who says he is certain he knows the location of the restaurant. After half an hour and three passes on the longest street in the city, and after asking every idle boda-boda and many who are not, we stop a besuited man on the side of the road talking into his cellphone. The man ends his call, dials the number from my slip of paper and gets directions. We had passed it twice already. The man shakes my hand, hands me his business card and says, 'If you are ever in need in Uganda, you must call.'

Later I take a boda-boda through the teeming streets to Mengo Palace, the seat of the Kabaka, or King, of Buganda, a monarchy that dates back centuries. The palace sits on a hill in ten square kilometres of grounds. I am picked up by a guide who has the heads-up look of a meerkat watching for predators. His English is not good enough for his chosen profession but, as Woody Allen once said, "eighty per cent of success is showing up" – so he gets the gig.

There is not much to see of the renovated palace, but within the grounds set into the hillside are a number of large concrete bunkers that deserve a closer look. The dungeons were used by Idi Amin, the buffoon-like dictator who ruled the country through the 1970s. However, dungeon doesn't come close to describing the horror that took place here. The torture chambers, accessible up a short ladder, are perhaps twenty-five metres deep by ten metres wide and ten metres high. There is no light. The walls of smooth concrete are covered in desperate pleas of innocence or defiance by prisoners who used charcoal, excrement and blood to write and scratch their hopeless messages or to make simple handprints – a legacy, a warning? – for future generations. One that reads, "I never forgot my husband was killed by people of Obote" proves that Amin's successor, President Obote, used the same bunkers to terrorise his own critics.

Amin seized power in a coup in 1971: he quickly became a grotesque poster boy for all that was wrong with African politics, and provided graphic evidence to Westerners who believed that Africa could not govern itself. It did not start out that way. Britain broadly welcomed Amin over the previous socialist regime. In fact, the British Army trained him.

In 1946 Amin joined the King's African Rifles (KAR) of the British colonial army as an assistant cook. He served with Scottish troops during this time, which instilled a lifelong fascination for all things Caledonian. He was transferred to

Kenya as a private and served in the 21st KAR infantry battalion until 1949. He was deployed to northern Kenya to fight against Somali rebels; then against the Mau Mau. His enthusiasm for fighting moved him up the ranks. In 1959 Amin was made warrant officer, the highest rank possible for a black African in the British colonial army at that time. Later, Amin returned to Uganda and was promoted to lieutenant, one of the first two Ugandans to become commissioned officers. Following independence, Amin was quickly promoted to captain and then major. In 1964 he was made Deputy Commander of the Army: that was when the power really went to his head.

Being from the northern Kakwa tribe, Amin concentrated his power by purging soldiers from the Acholi and Lango tribes, killing two-thirds of army personnel. Widespread massacres among the general population followed.

Following the coup that brought him to power, Amin set about wholesale expropriations of property and expulsions of ethnic groups that he believed were bleeding the country of its wealth, primarily Asians and Europeans. Indians, especially, were treated harshly. He said his decision to expel the 35,000 resident Indians came to him in a dream. He enacted the policy the following day. Asian businesses were handed to his supporters who often had no talent or interest in running the industries, and they collapsed. Amin then nationalised a string of British-owned businesses, which caused the already declining economy to disintegrate.

With little organised opposition, strong leadership turned into dictatorship. Parliament was dissolved, elections were outlawed, secret police exercised the power of life and death, the courts and the press were intimidated and subjected to severe repercussions for not toeing the line. Amin said, "I lead the country... how I want them to be led, according to my democracy, according to my knowledge and according to my thinking... No middle man."

He went further, organising public executions for those he thought were plotting against him. He felt threatened by journalists, artists, judges, lawyers, intellectuals and foreigners, many of whose bodies ended up in the Nile. Amnesty International estimated that half a million people were killed during Amin's eight-year presidency.

What makes his story so grotesquely compelling is that this butchery and sadism came from a character that played to the camera. His photogenic appearances and quotable jokes on TV news, his risible sporting claims, his immense physical strength and expanding waistline, all provided good copy in the West about the barely literate former Ugandan heavyweight boxing champion who bestowed on himself the title "His Excellency President for Life, Field Marshal Alhaji Dr Idi Amin Dada, VC, DSO, MC, CBE". He said his self-awarded CBE stood for "Conqueror of the British Empire".

His interest in Scotland and Scottish military regalia triggered his reference to himself as 'the last King of Scotland', whose aim it was to free the Scottish people from English subjugation. He once proposed marriage to Princess Anne as a way of patching up relations with Britain, then personally donated 10,000 Ugandan shillings to the old colonial master to help with the economic crisis in 1970s Britain.

But his jester-like behaviour was a blind. His wily cunning and ability to read and play people kept him ahead of his opponents and beyond the reach of international diplomacy. Western powers were not the only ones concerned; he was not well loved by regional leaders either. Uganda was landlocked and Amin coveted a route to the coast, which would have meant creating a corridor through Tanzania by force of arms. In 1972 he sent a telegram to Tanzania's President Nyerere, which read, "I want to assure you that I love you very much and if you had been a woman I would have considered marrying you although your head is full of grey hairs. But as you are a man, that possibility does not arise." Nyerere was not amused, and called Amin "A murderer, a liar and a savage".

Amin was ousted in a coup in 1979, and lived out the remainder of his life in exile in Saudi Arabia. When he died in 2003 he left six wives, several ex-wives, numerous concubines and more than forty children.

I leave the dungeons and walk up to a clutch of trees, close to where some families have made their homes within the grounds of the palace. There is a mass of mangled and rusting machine parts. The guide tells me they are the remains of a Rolls-Royce gifted by Queen Elizabeth to the King of Buganda, and later blown up – a perfect metaphor on which to end the day.

9

TOWARDS THE

MOUNTAINS OF THE MOON

Next morning, the trip goes on without a plan. As I get closer to Entebbe, on a whim I forego the opportunity to take the Lake Victoria ferry to Bugala Island, one of the Ssese Islands, and choose the road that leads further around the north-west edge of the lake. Later, with a chest full of diesel fumes and stinging eyes, I regret the decision. The highlight of the ride is a noisy roadside stop for a three-egg omelette filled with a chapati and grated raw cabbage. It's tastier than it sounds.

I pick up a newspaper and read a story about landslides that have been caused by torrential rain in Bududa, not far from my Kenya border crossing. Three villages have been destroyed, killing scores of people, possibly hundreds. Villagers were indoors when rivers of mud and rocks swept down hillsides, crushing homes and burying people alive.

After many days of inaction, rescue teams from the Ugandan army finally lead the search for survivors.

In 2010, landslides in the same region covered an entire village and killed about a hundred people. President Museveni, who visited the scene, rather unhelpfully said that the landslides were divine retribution for the villagers' failure to give back to the land what they take from it. There has been fierce resistance to relocation from villagers who refuse to abandon their ancestral homes, believing the government wants to designate the area 'a graveyard' and leave the bodies where they are buried, under the mud.

I find Bukakata, the nondescript ferry point on the lake's western shore that serves the Ssese Islands. Ssese is the local name for *tsetse*, after the infestation of the island by the flies known to spread a small parasite that leads to a potentially fatal infection in the brain, prosaically known as sleeping sickness. The pontoon ferry travels slower than walking pace and heads out like a creeping hand into the lake which, from this perspective, looks more like a sea.

The hotel on Bugala Island is bereft of life and sits in the gloom of the late evening; but a man offers me fresh tilapia from the lake, which is served with rice, chips and 'boiled Irish' (potatoes), so things are not all joyless. Before digging into the food, a waitress takes me by the elbow and leads me to a sink to wash my hands – and again after the meal.

Next morning I realise that, far from dreary, the hotel, located on a high bluff, has magnificent views of the lake and some of the other eighty-four islands in the archipelago. A boda-boda rider on the ferry yesterday told me that the islands were originally home to the Bassese tribe, although there is also a good sprinkling of incomers due to the good fishing and logging.

The air is uncannily still for such a high spot. Both malachite and pied kingfishers flit and dive, shoebills step through the grass like tip-toeing butlers, and a nursing vervet monkey with an upside-down infant clinging to her belly pinches grubs from the earth. Above me, still but alert, a buzzard surveys the scene with a cool eye. The only sound is a musical accompaniment from birds in the bush, perfectly tuned for an ear exhausted from the crash and din of Kampala.

The end-of-the-world air of this place is affecting. Like an island off the west coast of Scotland, the people are hardy and independent and probably view modern-day fripperies with disdain, such as internet access in Kalangala town, which is provided by a woman making clothes on a century-old Singer sewing machine who happens to have a laptop under her skirts. Pinned to her door is a poster showing a pretty girl above the headline, "You mean you are not circumcised! Stand Proud. Get Circumcised." It's a reminder that medics are struggling to control the staggering ninety per cent AIDS infection rate on the island.

Other slogans are hand-painted on school buildings: "Girls and Boys have Equal Rights; Education First, Others Will Come; Educating Children is a Collective Responsibility". Two girls lean out of a school window. Beside them, written on the classroom wall, is a list of warnings against getting into vulnerable situations: "Going to bars; Lonely places;

Free gifts and lifts; Visiting teachers' houses". Underneath, in blue, is chalked "Remember AIDS Kills".

On the beach I meet a guy from Wakefield, Yorkshire, who says he is disappointed every time he meets other white people in Uganda.

'I'm just saying, I'm surprised it's not all black!'

He describes his travels as if I haven't yet set foot in the country, and continues to prattle on long after the initial politeness has worn off. The Yorkshireman has the most recent copy of the Ugandan *Independent* newspaper with a splash headline about the government finally sending in a mechanical digger to recover the bodies buried in the landslides last week. Before that, the families of the missing were using spades and hoes to dig out their loved ones.

Approaching twilight, I push on to the resort's private beach: private to me and a catwalk of long-legged egrets, it would seem, as I am the only human visitor. I could be diplomatic and say that the resort on a beautiful bay with views to other islands wears its age gracefully like a fading film star – but I'd rather be honest, and say it's decrepit. The beach bar, with not a single bottle on a shelf, has a solitary lightbulb swinging above a girl who has her head buried in her folded arms on the bar. A man called Daniel arrives, who says that he is the general manager of both this hotel and its sister enterprise, the popular Lake Bunyonyi Overland Resort, close to the Rwanda border.

'I have three hundred people staying in Bunyoni,' he says. 'But here! Something is not working! I must find a way to fill my rooms.'

Next morning, my beach holiday is over. At 7 a.m. the dining room is empty as a crypt, and I trip over two staff seemingly expired on the floor of the kitchen when I go looking for food. There is only time to grab a banana before heading off for the early ferry back to the mainland. Accompanied by boda-bodas tearing over the loose surface, I skid through muddy villages that live in perpetual gloom under the forest canopy and don't get a chance to dry off before the next deluge. The minutes tick by towards the ferry departure as the forest seems ever more impenetrable. As I pick my way through a wrecked section of road, a boda-boda recklessly overtakes me with a passenger on board.

'The ferry is here,' shouts the rider. 'Be swift! Be brave!'

I open the throttle as far as I dare and brace myself for more violent bumps in the potholes along the broken-up surface. I pick up more boda-bodas who join the track from homesteads along the way with passengers and luggage hanging off the pillion seats. I reach the port and see the line of traffic waiting at a barrier. The last vehicle is being herded onto the boat.

'Your pass!' shouts a uniformed man at a barrier.

He selects a bank note from the handful I offer him and replaces it with a ticket.

Two *matatu* drivers are arguing with one of the boatmen who won't let them on this sailing, there's no room – but there is always room for a bike. I ride around the *matatus* and push my way through the passengers who are beginning to accept that they must wait hours for the next sailing. Before the boatman knows what is happening I am level with him, and continue up the ramp and onto the ferry. He shouts something at me, but I pretend not to hear and wedge the bike between two large trucks. I quickly jump off the bike and disappear. At that moment the ramp is pulled up and the ferry sets sail.

On the mainland I find some gratefully appreciated tarmac. I head south-east away from the lake in order to take a big swerve through Rwanda and Burundi. I plan to reconnect with the lake when I reach the Tanzanian shoreline.

After buying a litre of engine oil, I find a man who smells of hard work at a roadside stand in Mbarara, who charges the equivalent of 55p for a full bike service. After a brief but disappointing investigation of the town centre I decide to try my luck at the one upmarket hotel in the area, the Lake View Resort, a pretentious place three kilometres out of town. After a chilly boda-boda ride I fill up on the usual boiled Irish and *ugali*.

I get chatting with a Belgian called Gaspard who works for an organisation called The Refugee Next Door. He is helping to repatriate refugees and IDPs (internally displaced persons) who have either lost family in conflicts, or refuse to return to the scenes of their suffering. Most have come from conflicts in Rwanda and the Democratic Republic of the Congo (commonly known as DR Congo), but after spending years in Uganda, many are settled and wish to stay here. Others have fled northern Ugandan villages after they were attacked by the Lord's Resistance Army (LRA).

Gaspard says, 'We are trying to resettle a family of eight IDPs from Masese, near Jinja, to return to the north, their original home. You may have heard of the LRA: they attacked the Lango, Iteso and Acholi tribes who ran to the south and never returned. They are lost.'

The charity is very small considering the scale of the problem, but with people like Gaspard on their side, at least the IDPs have a mediator willing to open negotiations for their return.

'It is not easy to return people who have not been home for twenty years,' he says. 'Perhaps they are more settled here. We drove them north, helped them find a home and some land to farm. So far it's been a success, so we aim to help more people to move who wish to go home.'

That night the local spot cranks up the music at midnight and my bed trembles with the power of the bass speakers in the street. I've learned the lyrics to all the current Ugandan hits by 5 a.m. when the noise seems to wander off and get lost. I wake at 6.30 a.m. Breakfast is an unusual choice – even for Uganda – between either hot water in a flask, or pea and potato stew. I take the water and go begging for a teabag.

I take the road towards Kabale, a town on the Rwanda border. On the way I pass a group of men walking on both sides of the road, each carrying a piece of a butchered bullock: one has a haunch, another half a rib cage, while a small child swishes the air with the tail. The last man, holding on to the horns for balance, wears the bull's head like a bloody crown indignantly oozing blood and ouns.

For the second time in two days I overtake two European cyclists heavily laden with packed saddles and trunk bags. Up ahead I stop for a late breakfast on the road, and borrow a cellphone to call home. The line is crackly and I have to shout into the mouthpiece to be heard. My wife Olive's voice drifts in and out.

'HELLO?' I yell. 'HELLO?'

At that moment the lead cyclist is passing on the road and thinks I am shouting at him. He slows and rides up to me.

'I wasn't shouting for you,' I say, pointing at the phone. 'I'm trying to be heard in Britain.'

'No problem. I need to refuel. Breakfast!'

Soon the other cyclist rides in, closely followed by a minibus with two other white people in the front seats. Cyclists Pete and Julian are approaching the end of an epic ride from England to Kigali to raise funds for the Rwandan Olympic squad, whose team camp will be in Bury St Edmunds for next month's games. The cyclists are not far from their destination, after travelling through eleven countries and covering around 9,000 kilometres.

'There are three of us, but the other guy is riding at his own pace,' says Pete. 'We'll meet up before we ride the final stage into Kigali.'

The minibus parks up and out gets David, an American who runs a video production company in Nairobi and is recording the cycling trip for a documentary. The other white person (also American) is a rather glamorous woman who calls herself the film producer. She looks like she has just stepped out of a shampoo commercial. The mini film crew have been following the cyclists through Ethiopia, Kenya and Uganda. After a few moments comparing experiences in Africa, we are all fascinated by and envious of each other's journeys.

David, sunburned, with a week's stubble and wearing a sweaty scarf around his head, sticks his lens into the faces of the bikers and their plates of food, and fires questions at them to get them to open up on camera.

'Give me a break, David,' says Pete. 'Not while I'm eating!'

Underneath the beach-dude-on-tour look, David has one of those faces that I can't say is unfamiliar. But how?

'So, what's your story?' asks David, putting down the camera.

'Riding around the lake,' I say.

'I like it, man. Shit, that must take some doin'.'

'It's not difficult, but the seat gets a bit uncomfortable.'

'That's a cool bike,' he says. 'Wanna sell it?'

'When I get back to Nairobi.'

'When's that?'

'A few weeks.'

'I'll buy it,' he said. 'Keep in touch.'

He takes my notepad and writes his contact information next to his name: 'D David Morin'.

I've only just met David, but already I know that is a typically impulsive offer.

Keeping with the relaxed, cards-on-the-table atmosphere, I ask, 'So what's *your* story, David?'

'Simple. After years working in Hollywood, I realised what I was missing. One visit to Nairobi was all I needed to change my life. Change my *life*, man! I moved here and never looked back.'

'Would I know any of your films?'

'You might, if you're familiar with *CSI Miami* or *The Mentalist* or *LA Law*. I spent years acting in Hollywood. I had enough. Now,' he says, looking out to the hills beyond the village, 'this is more me.'

To add to the surreal nature of this interlude, the TV inside the restaurant is showing *Tusker Project Fame*, a regional talent show. Contestants sing songs to celebrate the joint 50th anniversary of independence for both Rwanda and Burundi. Contestants cover 'Waiting For the World to Change', 'Talkin' 'bout a Revolution', 'The Struggle Continues', 'Different Colours' and 'We Are the Future'. It's a great soundtrack to an hour of swapping stories, after which I leave the cyclists and crew to finish their meals and I take the mountain road south.

Kabale is a colourful mountain town at 2,000 metres that is colonised by a swarm of small motos carrying people about their business. As if I'd arranged it, I see a coffee machine on the stoop of a promising café. I can think of few things that I crave more than a real cup of coffee right now.

'Welcome to our coffee house,' says the winsome waitress on the verandah. 'What would you like?'

'It's a coffee house,' I say, unable to disguise my excitement. 'I'll have coffee! No, go mad, make it cappuccino!'

'We have no power,' she says. 'Maybe later. Will you wait?'

In a shared atmosphere of disappointment she brings a warm fruit juice and we discuss my onward journey to Rwanda. The easy option is to take the main road south out of Kabale and across the frontier, then ride the hundred or so kilometres into the capital, Kigali. Alternatively, I could take the road recommended by the Belgian aid worker I met in Mbarara. 'From Kabale,' he told me, 'head west to the frontier town of Kisoro if you want to ride one of the most beautiful roads in Uganda.'

No contest. I head west.

I join the end of a passing wedding parade of washed cars with streamers, and enjoy by proxy their sense of occasion as I set out on my last leg into Rwanda.

The road to Kisoro is a road I still dream about. The surface starts out smooth as marble but soon breaks up into gravelly unpredictability; then I am interrupted by small gangs of locals remaking the road with hoes and shovels. However, it does nothing to stop me marvelling at the spectacular route that hugs the waist of a mountain before rising steeply into the clouds. The patchwork fields and perfect terracing up and down the mountainsides look as if they have been arranged by an unseen presence laying a bedspread. Swarms of black and white butterflies rise up with my arrival and filter through me, some chasing me down the road, as swallows dart this way and that. Even at my sluggish pace I overtake exhausted trucks overloaded with goods for Rwanda that crawl in first gear up the relentless mountainside. With each new turn in the switchback road I get a fresh blast of ever-cooler air.

Then up ahead I see volcanoes in the densely forested Virunga National Park, the lush home of the silverback gorilla. Even though I feel I am already in touching distance of the sky, the volcanoes are soon towering over me, the clouds gripping their necks in a chokehold. Known for centuries, appropriately, as 'the Mountains of the Moon' by locals, the scene is almost unearthly, and feels as though I am getting to the end of something. The blissful scene leaves me with a warm heart and I don't want the ride to end. I am still riding it.

As if responding to the moment, Kisoro, the last town in Uganda, welcomes me with a raucous Christian revival meeting on what might be regarded as the village green. It's actually a football field in the centre of town, but that does nothing to inhibit the women in long yellow dresses and black sashes from injecting the town with a powerful injection of spiritual uplift. The music is so piercing, no one in the town could fail to feel part of proceedings.

Perhaps hoping for some more earthly entertainment, I choose to stay at the Graceland Motel. It's a dive, but a dive with a heart. The short man with little English who is tending bar greets my arrival with something that approximates hysteria. I can't fault him for enthusiasm. He shows me the stinking rooms out back and says, 'We have everything you could possibly need. One-stop!'

That's good enough for me – but even though he's already sold the room, he keeps selling.

'Room we have,' he says. 'Window is there. Food we have. TV in the bar we have. Extra pillow!'

I push the bike up an alley along the side of the motel and wedge it in a corner next to the kitchen. After I take a quick peek inside the kitchen door, I really wish I hadn't. I return to the bar where I find it difficult to find anyone who speaks conversational English. Perhaps the location of the town is the reason, wedged in the southwestern corner of Uganda bounded on two sides by Rwanda (ten kilometres south) and DR Congo (eight kilometres west). It is also less than fifty kilometres from the Bwindi Impenetrable Forest, home to the Batwa pygmies. They may have intermarried with people in the town, because I look like a giant here.

After a comically gruesome plateful of largely uncooked chicken and boiled Irish, the bar begins to fill up with Congolese from a nearby refugee camp and some who, at will apparently, meander over the border for work, shopping and girls. Tonight they are here for the Euro football finals about to be screened on TV. They do not mix with the locals and the atmosphere changes within a minute. Compared to the Ugandans in the bar (in fact, compared to anyone anywhere) the Congolese are wider, taller, more muscled and darker-skinned, which creates a spellbinding presence in the room.

As the bar gets crowded, it naturally divides down the middle, with the Congolese supporting the Ghanaian-born Mario Balotelli and therefore Italy by default, on one side, and the Ugandans who support Spain on the other. I am surrounded by the Congolese who squeeze up next to me on the bench seat. They are dressed in woolly jumpers and hats and drink from bottles and cans in plastic bags rather than buy beer at the bar. Nobody challenges them. One takes my uneaten, bloody chicken leg and chews it down to the bone.

It is soon apparent who the Congolese regard as their chief: a prodigious man with the largest face I have ever seen. He seems to be of a different species from the rest of us, moving awkwardly about the bar as if in a child's playhouse. He's everywhere at once. Ostentatiously he orders a bottle of beer and suggests making a large bet with the barman over the result of the match. The barman refuses good-naturedly, which initially I take to mean he wouldn't want to take the man's money; but perhaps he is aware of the risks involved in a financial transaction with him. Somewhat offended, the chief loudly slaps the money down on the bar. He has now grabbed the attention of all the staff. The barman reluctantly accepts the bet and slides the note, together with one of his own, under a jar for safekeeping. Now everyone is gripped in front of the screen. The chief takes a chair and, placing it in the centre of the floor, sits on it back to front, hugging the back like a precious thing.

Spain score first, which brings howls of derision and disappointment from the Congolese. People are yelling and arguing with the screen and each other. Nobody can hear a word the commentator is saying. Then Spain score again. Then it's 3-0. The locals know to keep quiet when Spain make it 4-0 and put the match beyond Italy's reach. The atmosphere turns sour as the chief picks a fight with a group of his own pals. He stands up, filling the bar, and directly threatens someone. Then he takes off his jacket and throws it on the floor. He is now centre stage and, from my seated position, he really is an impressive sight – but sight or not, I am looking for a way to exit without being noticed and before the man demands the return of his wager, which is now in the barman's pocket. There is a little space around him and the situation could go one of two ways: either the barman gives in and hands back his money, or the big guy employs a little Congolese muscle and demolishes the place. Alcohol comes to the rescue when one of his compatriots tempts him outside with a free can of beer. The bar takes a collective breath, and that is my cue to slip away to my room in the echoey courtyard behind the bar.

First thing, it is brilliant, cold and misty like a rare, bright October morning in Lancashire hill country outside Manchester. Villagers are wrapped up tightly in thin blankets and zippered jackets. Boda-boda riders, brave as flags, adopt stares of private tolerance and grit their teeth until the air warms up. Some have no gloves, so ride one-handed with the other stuffed into a pocket. Many wear hoodies, some outside their loose helmets, others inside together with baseball caps. To bring a little warmth to the street, the Victor Entertainment Centre opens for business by arranging two metre-high speakers at the door and firing them up with a recorded sermon – the first of many today, I'm sure.

A man steps out onto the verandah next to me. His voice is thick with sleep and he lights a cigarette. He is wearing pyjamas in better condition than the clothes worn by most people on the street. With a lost expression he gazes this way and that, as if deciding whether the day should be graced with his presence. Then, in an action of some decision, he steps off the verandah in bare feet and walks down the centre of the street, weaving between bicycles carrying children in tangerine and navy blue uniforms. A boda-boda rider carrying five children just misses him before he takes the hint and goes into a clothing store.

The barman, who I am glad to see is none the worse for his encounter last night, directs me across the street for food, which turns out to be the Mama Human Drug Shop. I must look worse than I feel.

Before I cross the border into Rwanda I come upon the Nyakabande transit camp for refugees fleeing the civil war in the DR Congo. I convince two armed guards at the gate to bring me to the administration tent. I show the Belgian aid worker's business card, but the administrator, who is a local with good English, doesn't buy it, and has no intention of allowing me to meet people or look around on my own. He keeps me close inside his tent and dispenses a few facts about the camp. He has the hurried gestures of a man running just ahead of a tsunami. He tells me there are 5,000 Congolese people living in the distinctive white United Nations tents laid out in perfect rows around us.

He says, 'They spend no more than three weeks here before transfer to a permanent camp.'

'So these people have been here for less than three weeks?'
'Yes.'

'Then another five thousand come in?'

'That is more or less how it works. If they stayed for longer it would not be a transit camp.'

'Where have they come from?'

'Anywhere within a hundred kilometres of the border, which is over that mountain,' he points, 'five kilometres away. The jungle is very dense and they have to get through the fighting. Of course, we do not know how many fail to make it. My job is to process the ones who do.'

I do a little mental arithmetic.

'So you process twenty thousand people a month. A quarter of a million a year?'

'It is so. Some have terrible stories. Sometimes they arrive still running from their pursuers who follow them over the border.'

I stand at the open flap of the administrator's tent and try to take it in. The ragged, the shoeless and the dispossessed shift among the rows of temporary shelter in the morning mist still sticking to the ground, the shadows of the volcanoes to the west giving the scene a surreal quality – but it's all too real for these people.

I take a few steps along the first row of tents. Women on the ground stir cooking pots, the only source of heat, while children huddle, squatting under tent flaps. One holds a spoon, another a broken toy. Men have a mercenary look. All are lightly clothed, which makes me shiver. The scene is multiplied down the row; the rows are multiplied across the plain. When there are so many people before you in such dire straits, the brain begins to compute in generalities. It estimates the number of people, approximates the colours and movement, and takes in impressions instead of hard facts, because the facts are not easily deciphered. It is called being overwhelmed.

The administrator takes a telephone call. A crowd locks into place when people get a sense that I might be someone of importance. A woman tries to hand me her baby and a man grabs me forcefully by the upper arm. I can't move. The administrator comes out of the tent and pushes people away.

'If you know what is good for you,' he says, 'you will leave now.'

10

TEA BREAK

In a few minutes I have reached what is possibly the most beautiful location in Africa for a collection of buildings of such mundane purpose: a border post. In front of me looms a volcano with a scarf of cloud trailing towards the east. More peaks recede into the horizon, making such human concerns seem insignificant. The clean air makes the colours of the fields, the sky and the dirt road look exaggerated, as if I am seeing them in a dream. The wind is a whisper.

As the sun warms up I try to shake off the experience of the refugee camp, and turn my attention to the handful of transients squatting in the dust waiting for papers to be approved; one moneychanger is doing slow business in no-man's land. The Ugandan customs officer, dressed in a black suit and tie, wants to keep the bike import document that I chanced upon at the Kenya–Uganda frontier. It is precious to me now and essential for the bike's passage at each frontier crossing. The official looks closer.

'This paper is mine to keep for your return,' he says. 'It says here that you must return to Kenya through Busia.'

He wants to send me back to the uniformed officer with the sense of humour failure on the Kenya border. I'd rather not. By pleading ignorance and creating a little confusion over the regulations, I convince him to make a photocopy of the document and let me go with the original. I don't tell him that I plan to go on to Burundi.

'You will see me again!' I lie. 'I have to return to Busia!'

I ride towards Ruhengeri through patchwork quilted mountains with blue peaks, volcanoes on my right and on the lower slopes, stick figures trudging up the steep sides. I'm not surprised they call Rwanda *Pays de Mille Collines* (Land of a Thousand Hills). After twenty minutes in the country I can confidently say that's not hyperbole. The road improves, and the first mountain villages look a little sturdier than the rag-tag Ugandan communities I saw on the other side of the border, and the Rwandan *matatu* minibuses (known locally as *twegerane,* Kinyarwanda for 'squeeze together') look as if they just might make it to the next major town. Lake Burera spreads out to my left with layers of mountains behind, and I see great swathes of low bushes laid out in military precision. Tea bushes, polished and glassy, are potently green and brimming like ripe vines.

Road signs – signs! – lead me to Ruhengeri, recently renamed Musanze, an adjustment common to many towns in an effort to obscure the old tribal associations of place names. Whatever it is called, the town is awash with bicycle boda-boda riders thumbing bells on handlebars to attract custom.

I stop close to the Dian Fossey Gorilla Fund International. The organisation, which organises anti-poaching patrols to protect the endangered primates, was founded by the American zoologist who spent much of the 1970s and 1980s studying the big apes. Her book, *Gorillas in the Mist*, became a bestseller and spawned a hit movie that was made three years after she was murdered in her mountain cabin in 1985. Despite many competing theories about the killer's identity, from poachers to government officials to an American research assistant, the killer has not been brought to justice.

Opposite is a pavement café and bakery.

'Coffee and cake,' I announce, when the waitress comes for my order.

'We have two kinds. Come inside and see.'

I leave my seat, go in and peer into the glass cabinet.

'What's this one?'

'Cake,' she says.

'What's that one?' I ask, pointing to the other option.

'Cake.'

'I'll take cake!'

She brings me out a cup, a flask of coffee, a small jug of hot milk and a slab of madeira-type cake the size of half a house brick. When two street kids come begging for food I break off most of the cake and hand it to them. One grabs it and makes to run off, but they both hesitate, perhaps because they think there might be more on offer. The woman from the café leaps out of the door and grabs the boy stuffing the cake into his mouth. A customer joins in the struggle and wrestles the cake from the boy. The two boys get away but the remainder of the cake ends up, mostly in crumbs, in the gutter.

Shocked by the severity of her intervention, I ask 'Did I do something wrong?'

The waitress disappears back inside with a look that almost curdles the milk on the table.

A customer who stayed out of the tussle says, 'We do not want beggars. We do not encourage, even if they are hungry. You are in Rwanda now.'

He picks up his cup and returns to his newspaper.

On the road to Gisenyi (now Rubavu) the air is cool and moist, and I ride for ten kilometres through tea fields. The afternoon is growing old before I see an advertisement that reads "Rwanda Tea, Ideal For the Whole Family". I immediately make a decision to visit the next tea estate. I get directions that lead me half an hour off the main road to a sign: "Rwanda Mountain Tea – Nyabihu Tea Factory". I ride in, but the factory yard is sleepy and there is only one man in an office near the front gate: factory manager Phillipe Nahayo. His response to my enquiries is one of polite indifference.

'The factory is still,' he says. 'There is a long weekend. You must return for the DG [director general]. He is in Kigali.'

'What time should I be here?' I ask.

'Seven-thirty in the morning. He will receive you.'

I ride twenty kilometres back down the mountain to Mukamira, a busy place with the main street filled with people carrying colourful woven bags on their way to or from market. Plastic bags are illegal in Rwanda, so vendors use blankets and boxes to carry, push or drag items to their stalls. Perhaps because it's market day that people here seem better dressed – and wear more traditional dress – than in what I saw of Uganda, and there is a convincing energy about the place.

I interrupt two *matatu* drivers arguing with each other over a fare to enquire about accommodation in the town. They both recommend what turns out to be the *only* accommodation: Sun Rise Bar and Lodging. Unfortunately, the Sun Rise is the sort of establishment where the sun has set and has not been seen for many years. The cheeriest aspect of the whole place is its name. There is a bar in a grim courtyard furnished with the ever-present plastic chairs, and a few rooms that open directly into the drinking area. There is a general store opposite playing music so loud that the woman who comes out to meet me has to shout to be heard. Madame quotes 10,000 francs (about £10) for a room. Cheap, but the frigid space with no water or power is forbidding. On the other hand, my intention was to stay as close to the tea estate as possible so I don't have a long ride in the morning.

Madame knows what I am thinking.

'The next town,' she says with little encouragement, 'is twenty kilometres.'

I gesticulate towards the music.

'When do they pack up and go home?' I ask.

'You do not like?'

'I like,' I say. 'I just don't want to feel like I'm on stage all night.'

'We can negotiate,' she shouts.

'I'll take the room.'

'Welcome. Let me show you what food we will service tonight,' she says.

At least I think that's what she says. Thinking she wants to show me the menu, I follow her into the empty dining room. On two fold-up tables in the far corner are six stainless steel trays. She lifts each lid in turn. Underneath is tonight's dinner, long cooked and already cold.

'Meat, boiled Irish, spaghetti, cabbage, sauce and beans,' she says.

All are swimming in liquid – in the parts where the fat has not yet congealed.

'Please choose,' she says, 'and we can make it hot for you.'

'Can you manage an omelette?'

'Yes.'

'With boiled Irish and vegetables.'

'Of course. It will be here in three hours.'

Later – four and a half hours later – after a frustrating time trying to locate the man who runs the internet office in town and who has taken the day off, I get a beef and onion omelette. I eat with two men who are chowing down on the cold hot buffet. When they get bored with the TV football, I change channels and catch BBC World on the scratchy screen. The lion's share of the news is about Tomboctou, which has been attacked by Islamic fundamentalists, Nigerian churches that have been bombed by people with a similarly chilling take on the world, and a report on South Africa's Jacob Zuma defending himself against various embarrassments. Then I hear David Cameron's name, which sounds like a reminder from a bad relationship, but I am not really gripped by the television. It is getting late and I am just putting off having to retire to the pit next door.

A security guard arrives with a heavy limp and a faraway look. It is an injury that is so severe, he might be better off losing the leg altogether. He is dressed in black boots and what amounts to a uniform. I'm not sure what help he would be as far as my protection is concerned. Perhaps he is armed. He watches me unlock my room and enter.

The room is cold, seriously cold. The concrete floor and walls seem to have absorbed it from a lifetime of chilly mountain nights. I have to leave the door open to benefit from the light coming from the bar at the other side of the courtyard. I try to shake off the gloom by arranging my things for the morning. There is nobody about, yet the music pumps regardless. I sit on the bed and notice it is dressed with only two threadbare sheets: one top, one bottom. Then a woman drifts over from the kitchen area and spends two minutes staring at me from the open door.

Eventually she says, 'Yes, I speak English.'

'Great. Do you have a blanket?'

Nothing.

'Blanket. To sleep under?'

I imitate a shudder and pick up the edge of a sheet.

'Ah! Sorry. I do not want to take from another room.'

Which seems a strange thing to say, considering I'm one of only two people spending the night.

'I'll need something,' I say, trying for a little sympathy. Empathy. Anything.

She leaves and returns with another sheet.

'*Je suis ici pour le petit déjeuner,*' she says.

Her English seems to have run its course.

'I here for your breakfast,' she says.

'Six a.m.,' I say. '*Six heures.*'

'Goodnight.'

As I push the door shut some late drinkers arrive. The combination of a courtyard full of echoey commotion and the brutal cold under the two sheets and my bike jacket makes it hard to drift off. I am woken by a noise in what seems like the dead of night. I check my watch: 6.30 a.m. I get up, hoping the noise is the breakfast girl. I peer into the gloomy courtyard and see the security guard twiddling the knobs on a transistor radio. He now has a pistol strapped to his good thigh.

Madame arrives as I am loading up the bike. She hugs herself in a thick bed quilt.

'I have come to make the warm water for your wash,' she says. 'Shall I make a fire?'

She knows the answer.

'It's too late,' I say. 'I have to be up the mountain before 7.30.'

With my left foot in the stirrup, madame issues the final indignity by indicating that I should push the bike into the street rather than start it up in the courtyard to avoid waking the staff. So that's what they're doing.

On the street, the few sleepy-eyed people who are up and about are doing the blanket-and-quilt shuffle. The security guard limp-skips after me and slams the gate shut as I fire up the bike.

Even though the sun has not yet risen, I am comforted by its promise, and look forward to the heat it will bring. And I seriously need warming up. By the time I reach the Nyabihu tea factory, the place is alive. Employees in broken shoes or wellington boots arrive at the gates on foot or on the backs of motos. The place feels like the beginning of school term as everyone returns from the long weekend. It is Tuesday 3 July today and I learn that Independence Day was Sunday just passed; Liberation Day is tomorrow, 4 July, which marks the eighteenth anniversary of the end of the genocide. The start of the atrocities is commemorated on Genocide Memorial Day: 7 April.

I introduce myself to everyone I can in an attempt to gain admission, but the word is that the DG is still in Kigali, and only he can permit access. Phillipe, the factory manager, arrives and is surprised to see me, even though he told me to be here. He indulges in half an hour of umming and ahhing, weighing up the first major decision of his day. Eventually – when he realises I am not going anywhere – he walks me over to the DG's office, which all the while has been occupied by the DG himself. Jean-Claude Murenzi speaks good English, but unfortunately he is a taciturn man who would rather listen than speak. What he does say is gladly received.

'Since you have travelled such a distance I see no reason why you should not visit my factory. Take as many photos as you wish, and drink our tea!'

Phillipe brings quality controller Josepha Umutomi to meet me. I am togged up in white coat and hat – matching hers – and given a tour that lasts most of the morning. On the noisy factory floor I am shown the delivery of tea leaves, then taken around the sorting, crushing, oxidation, rolling and drying machines.

Josepha says, 'The ratio of leaves plucked to tea produced is four to one. So the leaves get smaller as we go through the process.'

Finally I slurp my way through the tasting room and enjoy a variety of lip-puckering blends.

Josepha then arranges for estate manager David Sakindi to show me around the farm. David, dressed in black trousers, a zippered jacket and sunglasses, leads me down the mountain and inscrutably says, 'One bud, two leaves.'

He tells me that the region has been under tea cultivation since 1952, when the country was under Belgian rule. The tea bushes are laid out in perfect rows clinging to the mountainsides. We meet a swarm of pickers in among the bushes tugging at fresh leaves at waist height, as though wading in a green sea.

'One bud, two leaves,' David says again.

The pickers, who are not employed by the factory but rather pieceworkers paid by the basketful, carefully rip the fresh tops off the bushes and rhythmically throw them behind into wicker baskets carried on their backs. When I look closer I see that they carefully pick only one fresh bud for every two leaves.

'They have to work fast,' David says. 'They must return here in twelve days when the buds have grown once more. That is the plucking cycle – all year round. If it is wet, they grow even quicker. In drought, slower. If they pick too many leaves, the quality will not be good. If they do not pick enough buds and leaves, it will be a waste.'

A picker shuffles towards us. He lays a long wooden staff on top of the bush.

'This is a plucking wand,' says David. 'It is to maintain a flat plucking table. Any green leaf above that stick must be plucked. And so we have a uniform height throughout the estate.'

'How many pluckers work on the farm?'

'That depends on how many have turned up!'

David asks the lead picker something.

'He says there are seventy of them today, scattered around the estate. Tomorrow maybe more or less. There is no punishment if they do not arrive because they are like traders. They want to work; we want the tea.'

'How much do you pay?' I ask.

'Twenty-two francs per kilo; one sack weighs eight kilograms.'

That's about 16p per sack.

In the welcome warmth of the late morning we wade up and down the slope tickled by the thick tea bushes.

'Tea as far as the eye can see,' I say.

'The best,' says David. 'The high altitude of two thousand three hundred metres and the steep mountainsides make the best tea – and also because of the volcanic soil. It is here and nowhere else. That is why Rwanda has the finest tea: low yields, but the finest tea. It is more black and more flavoury than other countries. For instance, if you go to Kenya, you will find the Kericho tea a bit soft.'

'The whole mountain devoted to tea,' I say.

'Not all tea,' he says. 'Some Irish potatoes. The major cash crop is Irish; Irish everywhere. But the people must work, and if you are not working, life becomes an uphill task, like walking on the mountain.'

It is after midday by the time we walk back up to the factory. The factory manager tells Josepha to bring me a memento of my visit: two half-kilos of their finest tea.

Instilled with a solid feeling of belonging, I ride back through Mukamira and seem to meet every Rwandan I know: madame, the girl who brought me the extra sheet, the owner of the music-blasting general store, the man who came in on his day off to open the internet office, and two bar drinkers from the Sun Rise

Bar and Lodging. I've only spent one day in Mukamira, yet I already feel as though I could have a happy life here if I wanted it. I just need to remember to bring my own blankets.

11

'SOMETIMES STORIES GO ON PAST THEIR ENDING'

Although Rwanda is landlocked, the eastern border runs along Lake Kivu, so most of the country is within a few kilometres of a coastline. At the northern tip of the lake that sits at almost 1,500 metres altitude is the town of Gisenyi, from where I plan to begin a ride of the lake shoreline – if I can find a track.

I am accompanied for most of the day by other moto riders who usually spend time admiring the green bike ('You *militaire?*'), or racing me over the speed bumps in villages. However, because greetings take on a strict formality before a conversation may ensue, it can take a while to get to the nub of the encounter: for instance, asking directions while riding bikes side-by-side. It usually goes something like this:

Stranger: Good morning.

Me: Good morning.

Stranger: How are you?

Me: Very well, thank you. And you?

Stranger: Fine-fine.

Me: That's good.

Stranger: Welcome to my village.

Me: Thank you.

Stranger: May I help you in some way, *mzungu*?

Me: Which way to Gisenyi?

Stranger: You have passed it. It is now behind you, *mzungu*!

I need a day off to sort out my gear and allow myself to catch up with the ride. I try to negotiate an agreeable room in a lakeside hotel. The manager shows me a beautiful *banda* which, compared to the places I've stayed in so far, looks more like a honeymoon suite. The manager is insistent that he can't lower the price, but he will allow me to plead my case to the hotel owner, Mucyo. A mixed-race man in his mid-twenties, who is the epitome of politeness, steps out of an office. I'm in luck. As a fellow biker, Mucyo is predisposed to help.

He asks, 'How much can you pay?'

I give him a figure less than half the asking price. 'And I will eat here tonight,' I add, hoping the promise of a few extra francs will close the deal.

'Is fine. But not in the hotel by the lake,' he says. 'I have a house up on the hill. Overflow. You may look and decide.'

The manager slaps my palm and jumps on the back of the bike to direct me to three newly built hillside properties, one of which looks quite habitable. There is a little garden in front, and the one I am shown is spotlessly clean and has a view over the lake that is straight out of a travel brochure. We return to the lakeside.

'Is it good enough for you, the overflow?' Mucyo asks, with a smirk. 'Is the price fair?'

He laughs, and knows he has done me a big favour.

Later, the restaurant lives up to expectations, but throughout the meal I have to listen to a South African development consultant at a nearby table do his best to convince Mucyo that he should develop the site and the little peninsula opposite, to encourage more tourists.

'I don't think you realise what you're sitting on here!' says the South African. 'There's so much to be exploited!'

There is nobody else in the place, so when traditional dancers and singers wearing masks and straw headdresses arrive, I realise the South African is getting the full Rwandan treatment.

Back at the 'overflow', I am so relaxed that I fall asleep with the bedroom door wide open. I am woken by a grey cat that jumps on the bed and purrs in the moonlight. It is exactly how I feel.

Next morning I return to the hotel for breakfast, and take a table three metres from the lake shore. Vervet monkeys forage around me, and unseen birds chirrup and flit through bushes as a waitress brings fruit and fresh coffee, pancakes and honey. Two hundred metres across the water a perfectly conical hill rises on a spit of land. Like almost every other patch of land in this country, the hill is quilted with fields under cultivation. Just beyond it there is an uninhabited

143

island, the kind that might feature in a child's adventure story. A rowing boat propelled by four men straining at hoary oars completes the idyllic scene. Over the horizon is the DR Congo.

I get talking to the South African developer, Gert, who says he has been contracted by the Rwandan government to find three locations along Lake Kivu for tourist development. He gives me the spiel about the developments being eco-friendly and allowing locals to have first option to invest in the projects, but his words sound like PR gibberish straight from a prospectus intended to attract big-money investors.

Gert notices me taking in the view and says, 'This is one of our sites, man. If it is chosen, the government will compulsory purchase the land and move the small farmers.'

The combination of zealousness and indifference in his voice hits me like a stun gun. I wince.

'So, if I come back in ten years this place will all be changed,' I say.

'Two years! We hope to sign contracts very soon. If tourists come – the few that do – they just look at the view. Big deal! Then what? They stay a day or two and move on. But if you build resorts and develop attractions they will stay longer, spend more, and might return. It's obvious, man. The lake is so beautiful I know I will find my three sites somewhere on this coastline.'

Despite the dollar signs rolling in Gert's eyes, there is no doubt that Rwanda is underappreciated by Western tourists and could benefit from more growth (it has already been greatly helped by United Nations and European Union development money). If that happens, I hope the locals will benefit in more ways than just waiting tables and dancing in traditional costumes.

Gert, who has finally stopped talking long enough to admire the view, says that he is waiting for a boat to take him him south. It's two hours late and he wonders if it is the same one making its way lazily around the peninsula head. Mucyo joins us with a town planner from Kigali, and says that even he is not sure when or if the boat will arrive. Everyone stretches out and waits for someone else to make a decision. The atmosphere becomes languorous and still and nobody is in the mood to break the spell of the morning.

Then Mucyo's mother arrives and halts all conversation. She is a woman in her fifties for whom the word glamorous was invented. Odette is wearing a brilliant red full-length kaftan, black high heels, a gold necklace, bracelet and earrings which dazzle against her espresso-coloured skin, and has her hair brushed dramatically off her forehead. Dazzling too are her eyes. The Queen of Sheba comes to mind. The town planner's bottom lip nearly hits his shirt. I glance at Mucyo, who gives me a smile of recognition.

'Has everybody had enough?' she says. 'May I bring something more?'

I can see the town planner's mind working overtime. We're all still transfixed into silence by the striking sight of her.

'More coffee, tea?' she asks.

Me? Thinks the town planner.

I gather myself and think of something sensible to say. 'Your English is as good as Mucyo's.'

'Not only English,' she says, 'but also my own language, iKinyarwanda, Kiswahili, German, French. I was in Europe in the nineties.'

Clever too.

No one has yet noticed the man who accompanies the Queen of Sheba, I mean Odette. I think he is meant to be organising the boat for Gert for his exploit-the-coastline expedition. If he is, he's not in any hurry. The man, with a heavy accent, says he noticed my bike at reception and asks about the next stage of my journey. I tell him that I want to ride to Cyangugu, the Congo frontier post at the southern tip of the lake. He gets very excited and starts to describe something he calls the 'Con O'Neil Trail'. He points along the coast.

'You see, you see! The mountain?'

I can just make out a squiggly line of orange dirt heading up and over the hill that hugs the coast.

'This is your direction.'

He goes to his car and returns with a map of the "Congo–Nile Trail", a route along the shore that was designed by him for bikers and walkers. No wonder he's excited.

'Con O'Neil Trail,' he says, spreading the map over my breakfast table. 'Cyangugu is far, perhaps two days. Stop first in Kibuye. There are signs.'

'Not many,' adds Mucyo with caution. 'Keep within sight of the lake, which must always be on your right.'

As I'm packing up the bike, Odette hands me a few extra pancakes for the journey. She makes it feel like a personal assignation between us – at least, that's how I like to remember it.

I head off past the brewery on the lake shore and soon find the trail next to the Rambo Primary School (motto: "Knowledge, Patriotism, Work") up the side of the mountain. As I gain altitude I see tiny islands like humpback whales drowsing in the uncanny heat, and the dense tropical foliage perfectly framing the hazy view towards the archipelago and up and down the shoreline. As I ride higher the views become more spectacular, but still on a human scale. Among the bush are occasional villages and smaller homesteads and farms centred around mud-brick buildings and tight clutches of banana trees.

The trail starts out the width of two small cars, but in spots it becomes no more than a footpath; then it's the width of a single tyre through patchy grass. The trail closely follows the edge of the lake around tight bays and inlets, so that my direction veers from due south to due north and all compass points in-between. I'm probably riding double the length of the lake. Consequently, my arrival is rarely unexpected: it can be predicted five minutes before I arrive, because the tortuous coastline means people can see and hear me for miles. Because the trail is so narrow, my route interrupts whole villages at work or play. Children and dogs are primed to shout and bark and scamp alongside the bike; grannies are ready with outstretched hands; middle-aged men offer formal greetings; teenagers demand forcefully that I stop. I don't. The more remote villages come to a standstill and probably wonder, as one, *What is the meaning of this man's arrival*? A combination of the noise of the engine and the proximity between my wing mirrors and people washing, eating, playing or staring into space, makes me feel like I am trampling through people's lives. I do my best to offer friendly greetings and apologise for the disturbance, but it feels like I should have asked permission before arriving so rudely.

Mucyo was right: there aren't many signs along the trail, and I have to wait for people to point me in the right direction at every crossroads and fork.

I reach Kibuye by three o'clock and check into Home St Jean, a hotel perched like a sentinel high above the lake. At a raucous restaurant later that night I am welcomed by a receptionist with a nasty, star-shaped scar across his face and head. It is as if his temple was made of glass when it was shattered and the pieces only randomly fitted back together. The other side of his face is perfect and smooth. Then and now.

Every time I see someone in Rwanda over the age of eighteen who is limping or limbless or missing an eye or has some other visible injury – and it has been often – I privately speculate if their injury happened during the 1994 genocide. Were they *unlucky* enough to have suffered the blows of a machete; were they *lucky* enough to have survived? Whichever it is, they are here to tell the tale, and that tale must be told.

It is evident that the country is trying not to forget – at least not anytime soon – the murder of hundreds of thousands of people during 100 days of slaughter. The slaughter was predominantly executed by the Hutu against the Tutsis. But, of course, Tutsis have blood on their hands too. Most villages have shrines and burial grounds marked out by unmistakeable purple banners with the repeated phrases *Tuzahora Tubibuka* (We will always remember you), *Ntidigasubire* (Never again) and *Twigire ku mateka, twubake ejo hazaza* (Learning from our history to build a bright future).

I look closer at the broken man at the hotel. He is younger than I first thought, not much more than eighteen. If he is a maimed victim of the genocide, he must have been a baby. The dead are long buried but the injured, the survivors like the man before me, walk the country's roads to haunt the living of the time when the country lost its head and the world looked the other way.

Next morning I have breakfast overlooking the lake. I have another full day on the Con O'Neil Trail to look forward to and I feel as though nothing can spoil it. I engage with someone taking breakfast at the next table: he wonders why I should come to Kibuye. I would have thought it was obvious: the place is paradise. He says that the town was not always so. We both know what he is driving at.

'Tell me what it was like,' I ask.

I don't mention the word 'genocide' in case he changes his mind.

'You do not want to know,' he says.

'I do.'

'It is too dreadful.'

I gently insist. The tale spills out of him like marbles from a pocket. He tells me how the town trembled in panic at the first reports of slaughter coming out of Kigali, how the church across the way was used as sanctuary for fleeing Tutsis. He describes the venom that spouted out of the Hutu-controlled Radio Milles Collines, and the first man in Kibuye to be killed whose decapitated head was lofted on a pike at the town's roundabout. He tells me about the euphemistically named *Interahamwe* (Hutu militia death squads) call to arms, the machetes and tools distributed and used for weapons, the 20,000 Tutsis 'chopped' in the town, and the survivors who lived by playing dead for days until the stench of decaying bodies in the church was so bad that the butchers left for new killing grounds. Ten thousand people were murdered in and around the church on one day: 17 April 1994. The day this man, whose name I will never know, will never forget.

When he leaves a silence, I try to formulate a question, which is the most difficult thing I've had to do on this trip.

'Where are the killers? Were they caught?'

'They are here, my friend,' says the man. 'On the streets, here in Kibuye still. We must forgive.'

He tilts his head in a gesture of reflection and adds, 'That is part of what they call our reconciliation.'

I walk over to the reconsecrated church, a stone building with a bell tower. To one side of the front door is a memorial garden with a sign, in purple as always, that reads "Jenoside Yakorewe Abatutsi Muri Mata 1994" (Remember the Tutsi Genocide of April 1994). There are flowers wrapped in plastic on the ground and a clear window set in the wall, above which is written "Never Again". Above that is a crucifix. I walk to the window, and it is only when I come up close do I realise that the row of white objects behind the glass are human skulls.

The church interior is a single open space with plain, low benches in rows facing north, south, and west towards the altar. It is plain by the standards of Catholic churches in the West. What looks like new stained glass has been fitted into large window frames that dot the floor and walls in blocks of bold colours. Nearer the darker ceiling the light emits a deep, golden glow. Incongruously, bunting is stretched just above my head. I walk to the four corners of the church before I realise there is a woman kneeling in prayer at one of the benches. She doesn't look up.

I leave the sad and beautiful town of Kibuye and continue south towards Cyangugu. The trail is rougher than yesterday with fewer views of the lake, and I am put under even closer scrutiny by aimless children who materialise from the bush at every stop. It feels like I am being followed by the same group of kids armed with a collective attitude of belligerence, derision and fear, who stand exactly five paces from me. It matters not whether I stop to eat, check the map, rearrange my gear, take a photo or take a piss, they are there. I am the amusement, probably because there is precious little novelty out here. The villages, built into hillsides, are ramshackle at best and never fail to lower the spirit. The trail path often follows the steep slope of the mountain, so the rainy season must be an ordeal of flash floods, mudslides and inaccessible homes. The purple archways of memorial and reconciliation commonly seen elsewhere are replaced here by a simple arrangement of poles knocked up at the village limits. Gone are the familiar European Union and Red Cross signs common near Rwandan towns.

Ancient women bent double with milky eyes and knees like knots beg on the roadway, sometimes in the road. '*Un franc,*' they croak. One-tenth of a penny. I'm not sure if that will buy anything, or even if such a coin exists. It is difficult to refuse a grandmother. I don't. Further along, another crone raises a tiny fist in encouragement; I slow down and raise my arm, but then I see she has no fist, just a stump and a defiant glint in her eye.

Out of all this appears what could be a hallucination: a wedding party with bridesmaids in yellow and the bride in white, dust rising with every footfall towards wedlock. Then, as if offering a bookend to this high-spirited party, the next group I see are four men stepping down the road with curled banana leaves on their heads. Balanced on top of them is a plain wooden box, man-sized.

As the temperature soars I stop in Kirambo for some grilled goat and a bowl of beans. I get talking to a middle-aged man who is simultaneously drinking a bottle of Coke and a bottle of Fanta. I ask him for a translation of the banner at the village limit.

'It is a reminder,' he says.

'But what does it say?'

'It says "Never forget". But also "Don't remember". Don't forget the genocide, but don't remember who committed it. We are not Hutu or Tutsi now. We are only Rwandan.'

'That's a good attitude,' I say.

'We need attitude, yes, but also forgiveness because sometimes stories go on past their ending.'

There is nothing to add to such a poetic note. The only thing to do is to get up and shake his hand. I bring him my unfinished bowl of beans and he gives me a multi-gesture handshake. I want to ask if he is Hutu or Tutsi, but perhaps it doesn't matter as much as I think it does. If he was involved in the atrocities of 1994, as he surely was, either as perpetrator or victim, it is his story and it will go on long after its ending.

Towards the end of the trail I miss a turn, and end up on a wide stretch of road that is being levelled by a communal gang wearing street clothes, wielding hoes and make-do tools – which is probably an example of *umuganda*, an expectation that people will take part in public service once a month. Later, in a wide valley, I see hundreds of workers in a co-operative paddy field. There is little idleness here; sometimes it seems that every square metre of land is under cultivation.

Corn, bananas and rice give way to a huge tea plantation that puts an immaculate gloss on the landscape and marks the beginning of the end of two perfect days' riding. As I come off the trail I smell fresh tar, and ride onto a just-laid road. Work crews toil along the verges as slow-moving machines hog the centre of the road. The dotted white line is still wet. Villagers stand and stare at the new surface with looks of dread and wonder and pride; others wave and cheer as I purposely weave chaotically over the virgin, black road. Today I am the traffic. My mood turns to disappointment , however, when any hopes I had that the road was a wholly African project are dashed. I see two Chinese in Western clothing and hard hats shouting into their cellphones at the end of the thirty-kilometre stretch of infrastructure.

Next to a sign warning against child abuse that reads "Hakanira ba shuga dadi" ("Refuse the sugar daddy"), I turn into Cyangugu and find a hotel at the bridge that crosses to the DR Congo: a country ninety times larger than Rwanda, the smallest nation on the African continent. The Hotel du Lac offers me a 100-square metre room, the immense size of which compensates somewhat for no running water and no pillows. I hail a boda-boda to take me into the sister town of Kamembe to find an internet connection. The rider manages to send a text, answer a call and then make another while overtaking other boda-bodas before we've travelled five kilometres, mostly on an unmade road. It's a masterful demonstration of the art of multitasking.

I spend the evening in the dining room that time forgot, eating half a grilled chicken while listening to a young Irish aid worker speaking to two locals in a tortured form of pidgin English, which sounds like she is patronising two puppies.

Next morning I ride east through the Nyungwe Forest National Park, one of the largest mountainous rainforests remaining in Africa. It is soon apparent that development is forbidden within the park; it's eerily quiet. The familiar stalls, noisy street vendors and the beauty of village life are replaced with a perfect strip of tarmac that winds its way through the park. The best road in East Africa and no one is here. My jacket loses all its warmth and I can't stop shivering as I gain altitude to around 3,000 metres, but the jaw-dropping views down the tightly forested slopes are worth the chilly ride.

I stop at a lookout point that is inundated with L'Hoest's monkeys with their distinctive white beards. Above and around me fly double-collared sunbirds, dusky crimsonwings and streaky seedeaters. I can sound so knowledgable on birdlife because I meet Paul, a guide who has just returned from a three-hour hike with a party of Canadians. The last thing I want to do is make small talk with a group of white tourists, and anyway, the look they gave me when I arrived told me all I needed to know about my appearance after four weeks on the road. After sharing a bottle of water, Paul becomes the third person to make me an offer for the bike. Henry in Nairobi would be very proud.

Continuing east, I come upon Gikongoro, where a boda-boda cyclist leads me to the town's genocide memorial. I am soon to learn that of all the memorials, arches, burial grounds and churches devoted to the events of 1994, nothing comes close to the horror I am about to witness.

Alone, I stroll around the newly built visitor centre that fulfills the need to describe tribal perspectives to the killing, suggest some of the causes, explain the chronology of the slaughter and the non-intervention of the United Nations, and recount some personal stories. I am then asked to wait until someone comes to take me to the older buildings. A museum unlike any other.

An old woman, the kind of quiet and aged individual you only notice on second glance, indicates for me to follow her outside. We walk to the back of the museum in the fierce sun. Now I can see clearly that the site is on a low but steeply sided hill, with just one causeway leading to it. It is a magnificent spot. Each of the twenty or so similar hills within view are patched with tiny quilted fields clinging to their sides. Such is the clarity of the air, the hills seem within touching distance, but simultaneously I feel isolated on this stretch of ground. Slowly the woman heads towards rows of what look like windowless dormitories. In fact, the collection of buildings used to be a technical college; but no longer.

With a heavy heart, the woman explains something to me in French. An awful massacre happened here, she says. She will never forget. I don't catch all that she says, but one phrase, *'Toute ma famille ont été assassinés,'* stands out. I latch onto two words: 'family' and 'assassinated'. She doesn't have to say any more; but as if saying a mass, she continues until we reach the first building. She stops at the door of the first classroom and, with emphasis, says, *'Photographie interdite,'* then indicates for me to look inside.

The room is about eight metres square with two rows of wide, low wooden benches on which appear to be laid broken white mannequins; twenty or thirty there are. Large and small and tiny, full-size and half-size and doll-like. Adult, child, baby. The bodies, some whole, some in pieces, are dusty white with lime. Despite their shattered limbs and having a look of disarray, they seem at the same time to have been lovingly placed. They have been saved from total decay by the action of the lime, so the bodies appear to have risen from fresh graves. Some have the remnants of clothing draped around twisted limbs, others have tufts of matted hair sprouting from smashed skulls. Muscles are stretched and tendons snapped, necks are twisted in depraved torment. Babies lay next to mothers, sisters and brothers spoon up like they're taking a nap. Some bodies are flattened, no doubt from the action of interment. For these bodies have been exhumed from a pit outside the school, a pit for Tutsis dug by Hutus to hide the evidence of their crimes.

The old woman is silent. I say nothing. I have seen, I cannot unsee. When my eyes have taken in everything I can stomach, I glance at the woman. She makes a grab for the end of this elastic moment by clasping her hands together and loudly praying. When she has finished she leads me to another classroom. I am thrilled to be outside for a few seconds and look up to the picture postcard hills to regain some composure. I take a guilty breath, but the air has a new unhealthy tang to it. I recognise a kind of numbness in me, nothing that could yet be called feeling.

As if sensing the movement of my thoughts, the woman says that the bodies were exhumed from a mass grave close by, then displayed in the very classrooms where they were slaughtered.

'*Photographie interdite*,' she repeats, and brushes her hand towards the next door.

There are more children's bodies here, less decayed, expressions of agony still visible on faces, anguish still present in tiny fingers. Another classroom of cabinets and trestles displays rows of body parts. Yet another has skulls laid out according to size. We reach the end of the first row of classrooms and the woman leads me to the next. A hundred exclamations come to mind, but none of them come out. I want to say *Enough, more than enough* – but she is showing me the last resting place of her entire family. How can it ever be enough? I enter a room of bodies that look eerily fresh, ready to pull off the white masks and speak to me; others have their heads raised off the bench as if questioning their predicament. *Is it not time to return home?* The bodies that are most pitiful are those largely intact with a missing foot or hand, or a single cleave to the head. What did they witness? What were their final thoughts?

These are the bald facts of the story. When the killings began in April 1994, Tutsi families in the region fled to Gikongoro, which was regarded as a safe haven. The authorities directed them to the technical school under construction on Murambi Hill, a short distance outside the town. The 40,000 Tutsis who fled here were promised protection by a contingent of recently arrived French troops. However, soon the Hutus cut off the water and electricity supply. Then food became scarce. Rather than being protected, they found themselves exposed on the hillside.

The Hutus had them where they wanted them. For five days Tutsi families were terrorised by gangs who surrounded the hill and attacked by night. Weak with hunger and thirst, the Tutsis did their best to defend themselves with stones and sticks, but the terror gangs were just a precursor to the main event: the heavily armed *Interahamwe* ('those who work together'). They arrived on 21 April and clinically went from classroom to classroom, shooting and hacking down everybody they could find. Next morning they scoured the hill for those who managed to escape and killed anyone not yet dead, leaving almost no survivors. Then the killers brought a tractor to dig a mass grave for the bodies. A few Tutsis survived by playing dead and making their escape under cover of darkness. Modern-day estimates of the dead range from 40,000 to 50,000; many graves have not yet been discovered.

Two years after the genocide, the remains of 5,000 victims were exhumed. Most were reburied but almost 1,000 bodies, some eerily well preserved, were dosed in lime and arranged throughout the abandoned school to bear witness to that night in 1994.

The old woman continues to pray with the air of doggedness that she's worn all afternoon, for the past eighteen years maybe, as she walks off back to the museum.

This gruesome display is an essential part of national remembering, because even now some Hutus do not accept that such atrocities took place. Others refuse to finally bury the dead by never wishing to bury the memory. How do you deal with such a knotted ball of trauma? Do you tease it out over time? Or cut it?

Modern-day Rwanda, the most densely populated country in mainland Africa, is a conundrum. As much as I want to say there is a sense of balance between the atrocities of 1994 and the industry and forgiveness there is everywhere around me, it is impossible to reconcile the savagery of the country's recent past with the present peace. In fact, more than peace, Rwanda is outwardly one of the most placid African countries I have visited. Nothing can balance what happened in those 100 days, but it would be churlish to ignore the sense of potential and opportunity in this country. Inspiration for the future comes in different forms: the 1,000 people working in the road crew; the co-operative paddy fields; the European Union and United Nations aid; the fact that Hutu and Tutsi walk side-by-side down every street in every village.

Despite the ostensible progress, post-genocide Rwanda was not easy to rebuild. Following the defeat of the Hutu militia by Tutsi forces, many perpetrators were imprisoned; others fled to the DR Congo and Burundi. So many people were implicated in the violence that the justice system was overwhelmed. The new government, led by the enigmatic Tutsi Paul Kagame, eventually created a nationwide network of Gacaca courts: a form of community justice where victims had their say, and perpetrators admitted their guilt and described the details of their crimes. While not all have been forthcoming in their disclosures, many convicted killers have returned to their villages and now live among the families of those they butchered.

There is an interesting background to the divisions between Tutsi and Hutu.

Rwanda was little known outside East Africa before the genocide. The first European to mention Rwanda was John Henning Speke in 1863, relatively late in the continent's 'discovery'. The German explorer, Count Gustav Adolf von Götzen, did not reach Lake Kivu (the country's western boundary) until 1894, by which time Rwanda had become part of German East Africa. The Germans favoured Tutsis as a superior race because of their generally taller stature, more European appearance, readiness to convert to Roman Catholicism, and what they saw as a willing and trustworthy demeanour. Consequently, Tutsis were given positions of authority in the new colony, while Hutus remained farmers. This hierarchy was acknowledged through interpretations of the Bible that propagated the Hamitic hypothesis, which suggested that some Africans were descended from Noah's son Ham. This myth was promulgated by Speke, who used it to explain the difference in physical characteristics between Tutsi and Hutu. Commenting on the Tutsis more Caucasoid facial features, he asserted that Tutsis must have descended from Ham and migrated from the far north, while other races were negroid and came from what he termed "barbaric civilisations". This perception of innate superiority and inferiority persisted – perhaps that is when the trouble began.

Belgian troops seized Rwanda from Germany during the First World War. Then the Belgian Congo and Rwanda-Urundi were unified in 1925. In an socially divisive action, Belgian ethnologists analysed thousands of Rwandans in order to establish racial differences. In a move that would be copied in Nazi Germany in the following decade, identity cards labelling each individual as either Tutsi, Hutu, Twa or 'Naturalised' were introduced. Today, ethnic classifications are not displayed on official documents.

I leave Murambi Hill, but it's fifty kilometres before I feel I've really gone. The savage legacy of the college classrooms and the old woman praying amid such sublime countryside creates a dissonance in me that could probably only happen in Rwanda. At times like these, when I have thoughts that cannot be easily ordered, the road becomes a balm, a self-perpetuating reason to continue.

12

HOTEL RWANDA

I ride to the university town of Butare, now officially renamed Huye, then on to the capital, Kigali. I find a cheap hotel that is not cheap enough and spend ten minutes haggling with the receptionist, to the amusement of a young English guy looking on. The price of the room is finally trimmed and I take it, mostly because I don't have it in me to go through it all again somewhere else.

In spite of the experience in Gikongoro, I am compelled to go to the Kigali Genocide Memorial. In contrast to the stark buildings on Murambi Hill, it turns out to be an elegant and reflective shrine with a rose garden and poignant works of art. The exhibits inside tell harrowing stories that explain the lasting effects of psychological trauma, the overwhelming number of orphans left by the mass killing, and the legacy of AIDS following the widespread rapes during the 100 days of madness. Close to a million people were murdered and one million fled to neighbouring countries in 1994. The shock of that upheaval to social cohesion, village life and the national economy was profound. Every family must be able to name one of their own as either victim or perpetrator. The blemish of guilt stains everyone. Despite the obvious need to tell these stories, I can't help being troubled by the feeling that the explicit nature of the memorial – and the gruesome one at Gikongoro – feeds the commonly held Western notion that Africans can be especially brutal to each other and disregard the sanctity of life when it suits. Beastly Africans. When it rains in Africa, it floods.

One room is devoted to children. The pathos of the exhibit is too much for many visitors. Tears are the only response. Beneath a photograph of each young victim is a stark summary of the child's short life. One such reads:

Name: Nadia Chanelle Ruterana Kanuyange

Age: 8

Sport: Jogging with her father

Sweets: Chocolate

Drink: Milk

Saying: My native land which God chose for me

Enjoyed: TV and Music

Cause of Death: Hacked by machete

Outside I am faced by another incomprehensible statistic. Before me there are rows of mass graves, each perhaps twelve by thirty metres, the final resting place of a quarter of a million people who were slaughtered in Kigali.

As I walk back through the rose garden past the graves, a fig falls from a tree not thirty centimetres from my face. I just fail to catch it. I have found Rwanda equally unattainable, just out of reach. For all its present hope and expectations, it hides a sadness that will remain in this soil for generations. My response to the country is unlike any I have experienced in Africa. I feel like there is something in my life now that was never in it before. I am surrounded by victims, but also heroes. In some way we all need to be heroes to ourselves at least once a lifetime, even if it's in death.

There is only one thing to do. I need a drink.

I ride to the Hôtel des Mille Collines, a characterless slice of four-star luxury set in lush gardens on a rise overlooking the city. In 1994 the hotel became a place of refuge when the manager, Paul Rusesabagina, who was born to a Hutu father and Tutsi mother, risked his life to shelter 1,200 fleeing Tutsis in the hotel and grounds. He told the story in his memoir, *An Ordinary Man*, later filmed as *Hotel Rwanda*.

At the entrance a man poses for a photograph, which is being taken by a ham-fisted security guard.

'Just visiting?' I ask the visitor.

'There is a history behind this photograph,' he says cryptically.

'I'd love to hear it,' I say. 'Let me buy you a drink.'

We walk through the bland reception to the welcoming swimming pool – the first I have seen in Rwanda – with a boma bar. Almost every drinker in the place is white. We take a seat at a table near two televisions, one showing Bradley Wiggins winning the Tour de France, the other showing Serena Williams winning Wimbledon. Between them, the English guy I saw in my hotel reception is drinking heavily at the bar.

I order beer. Juan, my putative drinking buddy who now says he is teetotal, orders fruit juice. Originally from Mexico, Juan was educated in Washington, DC but now lives in Canada after spending most of his life travelling the world. He tells me he is a human rights lawyer working for the United Nations in South Sudan, the newest country in Africa and due to be granted its official independence in two days' time. He says the country is in a state of turmoil and that he can get nothing done without the liberal use of hard currency.

'I am living in Juba, the capital, in a container,' he says, 'because there are no buildings following the civil war. No buildings! I do not exaggerate. If you want a basic room, African basic, it will cost you US$100 a night. It is like the Wild West.'

'Sounds hectic. Why are you here?' I ask.

'I come to Kigali every six weeks or so for some R&R. Most UN people come here. It's handy, there's good food and most things work.'

'So, what's your connection to the Mille Collines?' I ask.

'I used to live in this hotel, shortly after the end of the genocide. I was sent by the UN to help with reconciliation and repatriation and the desperation. The city was a mess. The survivors, the dispersed, didn't want to go home because the people who murdered their families, the *Interahamwe*, were still roaming the streets. How *could* they go home?'

Inappropriately on cue, the house band plug in and start their set with a reggae version of the power ballad 'I Want To Know What Love Is', but nothing will interrupt Juan. He responds to my upbeat interest in his working life as an excuse to lecture me on the pitfalls of international diplomacy and the shortcomings of African governments. I just want a night off.

I catch the eye of the English guy at the bar and invite him over, for no other reason than for a bit of variety. He is already having a good night out: a one-man party. Our new companion, Tom, is from another branch of the Westerners-helping-Africans industry. He says he is spending the summer building a school in Uganda, arranged through a British volunteer organisation that sounds more than a little chaotic. He is in Kigali for the same reason as Juan.

Very quickly it is clear that my two new friends have absolutely nothing in common, and both rely on me to keep the conversation going. Juan is sober, serious, well-travelled, well-read and wants to talk politics. Tom is getting drunk, finds a hole in every thread of conversation, and has a knack of laughing inappropriately. Even though I am already fairly merry myself, the glass before me always seems inadequate.

Juan finds an excuse to stay at the bar as I take Tom back to our hotel, lock up the bike, then hail two boda-bodas to take us to a pizza place. It's really the only thing that will do. Tom and I are feeling a little heady and, with the cool wind rushing in our ears as we speed up and down the hills of Kigali, we try to push each other off the pillions. The boda-

boda riders don't seem to mind, and soon get into the spirit of things by racing each other to the restaurant.

Now that Tom is not competing with 'Mister Travelled-the-World', as he calls Juan, he relaxes and talks about his experiences as a volunteer. He is keen and sharp, but feels his talents are undervalued at the charity project and criticises the way the organisation is run.

'Too much time is wasted,' he says. 'When there is labour, there are no materials to build. When we have materials, no one shows up. My eyes have been opened to Africa's problems. I came with the best intentions, and I'm afraid I'll end up like most people who volunteer: realise they can make no lasting good, and treat it as another holiday. I hate my job back home, so I hoped this was going to be a life-changing experience. The only saving grace is the old woman that I live with, my host mama. She gives me a bed and feeds me in return for pennies. Full board costs the equivalent of two pounds fifty a night! I spent more than that on each beer at Hotel Rwanda this evening. It's crazy. I wish I could come back on my own at some point. I could achieve more in a week than I could in a month with the outfit I'm with.'

For me, once the pizza is eaten, the night has run its course. We get back to our hotel and Tom staggers into the bar to continue drinking. I go to my room and pack up ready for an early start.

13

'NIGHT IS NEAR, AND
NIGHT IS UNSAFE'

Next morning, after an oil change the bike more than deserves, I retrace my steps on a narrow and winding road 150 kilometres back to Butare, then continue south to the Burundi border. There are fewer people here and they are quieter than those nearer to town, which unnerves me. I'm more used to people waving me down or trying to sell me something grilled or a bunch of bananas or as I ride by. The mountain backdrop is spectacular, which accentuates the shabbiness of the people on the roadside. The road drops off the mountain to a ragtag border post with an air of menace. Sweating women with sacks on their backs and dirty men with trucks parked on the verge simultaneously argue with an official behind a grill. When they get a stamp in their papers, they remain at the window to argue some more.

Before the barrier, the Rwanda flag flutters above the little customs building. The cheerful sky-blue, yellow and green horizontal stripes and shining sun that I have grown accustomed to seems to flap farewell.

I have one brief interaction with a man whose car is almost rearing on its hind legs, so packed is its open boot.

'Burundi?' he asks. 'Don't go.'

But go I did.

On the Burundi side, the road rises steeply and soon I am treated once more to hazy panoramas of deep valleys and perfect conical peaks. What few road signs there were are now behind me. Something more is missing, though. In Rwanda these hills would be carpeted with fields laid out in neat rows of vegetables and corn or Irish potatoes, but here the mountainsides are still wild. Meanwhile the roads are narrower and twistier, so much so that it is difficult to overtake even the slowest vehicle. Container trucks struggle up inclines with a score of people clinging to the back for dear life, while cyclists hold on and get a free ride up the hills.

It only takes a ride into the first village to confirm without question that I am now in one of the world's poorest nations. The collapsed villages and towns are desperate places. People often wear rags instead of clothes, and where they have clothes they are simple robes. The villages – chaotic collections of crumbling homes – display no paint, have no obvious shops, no advertising or brand names, just the dun colour of mud-brick structures strung out along the muddy road. People are commonly barefoot, and greet me with cracked, calloused hands outstretched as if in wonder.

What was mechanised in Rwanda is here achieved by crude labour: tyres are pumped by hand rather than with pneumatic air lines, handsaws in place of chainsaws are pushed and pulled through planks, knotted banana leaves or palms are used to carry staggering weights of charcoal or fruit when they're not pushed on bicycles up the mountainsides by men leaning against handlebars. The ubiquity of cellphones in other parts of East Africa now becomes apparent in a region with few devices. I notice a couple of projects funded by the UNHCR (United Nations refugee agency) and a coffee washing station built by the European Union, but by and large Western help, and all its consolations, hasn't yet arrived.

The only outward display of cheerfulness I see comes from women who wear shocking multicoloured headdresses in the national colours of red, white and green, often matched by umbrellas twirling on shoulders. Where Rwandan women took great care over elaborate and eye-catching hairstyles, Burundians often have shaved heads with a short, flat top. Strangely, the people who wear shoes seem to be shod in either lime green or orange plastic sandals, which can be seen flip-flopping a kilometre away.

People are truly astounded to see me. Some gape open-mouthed, but most teenagers and young men shout aggressively. Older people beg, it is true, but it is usually with an expression of hopelessness, and none of the weary mockery I have come to expect.

I reach Bujumbura, the capital, known as Buja, by five o'clock. The welcome is not as I'd hoped. The suburbs, such as they are, suck me into a vortex of catcalls and threats in the city centre. Men lean out of *matatus* or run into the street to accost me and strike the bike just for being there, to sell me something, to change money, or to utter an oath. There is a worrying number of weapons on display – mostly ones that fire bullets – and each time I stop to check the map or look for someone who speaks English, I get intimidating interactions that impel me to flee. The belligerence never comes from just one person; if someone approaches me, they quickly rouse a crowd.

I am overtaken with a sense of urgency to find accommodation before nightfall. I locate a small hotel with an armed guard on the door – which is far from remarkable, as *every* shop and hotel of any consequence has an armed guard on the door. I remember only one thing the receptionist says: 'Night is near, and night is unsafe.'

There are few street lights on when I go out looking for food after dark. I offer a taxi driver 2,000 francs (about £1) to take me to a restaurant recommended by the hotel receptionist. Rather than suffer the dark silence in the back of the taxi, I try a little conversation.

'How is Bujumbura?'

'Is good. Before?'

'No, first time. I hear it is dangerous. Is it secure?'

'No. Secure, no.'

He mumbles something and taps the glove compartment of the Nissan and glances back at me.

'Is okay,' he says, knowingly. I know what I am meant to believe. That he is armed, and is prepared for any situation.

The restaurant is closed but I see there is a curry house next door which has plenty of customers, so ask him to drive onto their property where there are more armed guards at the gate. I hand the driver the agreed 2,000 francs and bid him goodnight. He says the money is not enough. I get out of the car and check the note in the beam of the headlight: BIF 2000. He knows the value of the note, but he wants more. He becomes aggressive and steps out of the car to face me down. He refuses to accept the money, so I leave the creased and torn note draped on his open door and walk into the outdoor restaurant.

By this time we have caught the attention of the waiters; one guides me to a table while another tackles the irate driver. I am happier with the six-foot waiter between us. I indicate that the argument is over, and order a beer. The waiter explains that the driver wants more because he took me to a different address, so the agreement to take me next door does not stand. The driver is still arguing with the other waiter, pushing him and gesticulating in my direction. The armed men that I believed were guarding the restaurant have long made themselves scarce. All the customers, a minute ago up to their elbows in poppadoms and chicken masala, are now involved, whether they want to be or not. Some look over with noncommittal expressions, others comment on the escalating situation under their breath. In plainer moments this disagreement would have been solved in seconds, but there is something in the air. Something ugly. I have been pushed into the position of patronising and duplicitous European, which I now regret.

With a hammering heart, I begin to believe the driver is capable of anything. The more the odds are stacked against him – the waiters, the setting, the sight of wealthy *mzungus* eating curry, his own injured dignity – the more my mind considers what might be stashed in the glove compartment of the Nissan. Very quickly he could make it clear how he is feeling.

Another waiter gently takes him by the arm, but he is having none of it and rushes towards his car. He sits in the passenger seat and stares out at me. After scanning the restaurant for a back exit, I call over the waiter and say that although this is not the time for me to go over and negotiate with the driver (as my very existence is what's infuriating him), we have to calm him down somehow. The waiter offers to give him another 2000 francs, and add it to my bill, a compromise with which I readily agree. The driver takes the money, hurls some more abuse in my direction, and leaves.

All that for a chicken tikka.

Burundi is landlocked. Tanzania lies to the south and east, Rwanda to the north and the great Lake Tanganyika runs along most of its western flank. Further north, it shares a border with the DR Congo. Look at an atlas: if you can find the tiny country hidden in the centre of Africa, you will see that the outline of Burundi is the shape of a human heart. But it is a heart that has been broken many times over its short history since independence.

Like Rwanda, Burundi has suffered simmering tension between the Tutsi minority and the Hutu majority since colonisation by the Germans in the late nineteenth century. The two countries once functioned as a single colony known as Ruanda-Urundi, before gaining independence separately in 1962. Social differences between Tutsis and Hutus have contributed to political unrest ever since, leading to lengthy civil wars which killed hundreds of thousands of civilians in the 1990s. The Tutsi–Hutu strife made Burundi a de facto player in the Rwandan genocide, providing sanctuary, arms and fighters to both sides. "Reconstruction" is supposedly under way in Burundi, and there is a peace of sorts between the government and most of the splintering rebel groups, but tensions remain. The most recent unrest occurred after the 2010 elections, which renewed fears of another civil war, and prompted the British Foreign Office to advise against all but essential travel. I shouldn't be here.

Wars and poor governance have left Burundi in an unenviable club: that of the world's five poorest nations (nineteen of the bottom twenty are in Africa). Burundi is at, or close to, the very bottom of every poverty indicator: gross domestic product, earnings, malnourishment and access to health and education. In a strange way, it is a relief to know how Burundi compares to the rest of the world because, now that I have seen it with my own eyes, I would hate to think that anywhere else was worse.

I spend a fitful night arguing with the taxi driver in my head while the curry has an argument in my stomach. Next morning, the image of him sitting in the passenger seat of his scabby car at the restaurant returns and leaves me cold.

What was he contemplating? What were his options? What would he have done for the extra £1?

Bujumbura is beginning to worry me. After easygoing Rwanda, the city is the equivalent of a stiff drink after months of abstinence. The morning headache tells me I should leave town. Even though I have been told that the areas surrounding the city are more dangerous than these mean streets, I can't help feeling that I will be happier in the wilds – and with a following wind, I may just make the Tanzania frontier in one day.

A few kilometres south of the city there is a spot that claims a place in the history of European exploration. Not far from the main road, near a river winding its way down to Lake Tanganyika, somebody has marked a boulder taller than me with the inscription: "LIVINGSTONE STANLEY 25 XI 1871". The place marks the visit by Livingstone and Stanley. It is a peaceful, beautiful spot, despite my visit prompting the arrival of a posse of children and teenagers keen to try on my helmet. Livingstone came to Africa as a missionary determined to spread the word of God and build schools, but it is remarkable how few schools I have seen in this country. There are too many children on the roadway looking for an education.

Some claim this is the place where Stanley 'found' Livingstone. That historic meeting, however, happened fifteen days earlier and about 250 kilometres down the lake shore in Ujiji, Tanzania.

The first Europeans to see Lake Tanganyika – the second largest and second deepest freshwater lake in the world –

were Speke and Burton, in 1858. I say 'see', but Speke was temporarily blind at the time and could not properly discern the lake. This occurred on the same expedition when Speke went on to discover Lake Victoria and identified it as the source of the Nile. The two men had travelled together before. Their first expedition together, in 1854 to Ethiopia, was a disaster. Speke was almost killed by a hostile tribe after being captured and stabbed several times before he was able to escape. In the same attack, a spear impaled both of Burton's cheeks. He escaped with the weapon still in his mouth and bore the impressive scar for the rest of his life.

On their second journey the two adventurers returned to East Africa to look for what they believed to be the Great Lakes. They suffered again for their curiosity. Both men caught tropical diseases, and Speke became temporarily deaf after a beetle crawled into his ear and he tried to dig it out with a knife. Real *Boy's Own* stuff.

The lakeshore road is a joy. However, even though I am riding through a landscape that takes my breath away, the overwhelming feeling is one of claustrophobia. I am tempted to take a dip in the lake, but every time I stop I am mobbed by watchful people who appear from the bush like soup through a colander. The little country is so crowded there is not a lonely stretch anywhere. The villages have little to recommend them to a passing visitor, just crowds of people parting the roadway like excited spectators at the Tour de France. Then I see something remarkable, something man-made: a chimney, smoke, a warehouse and the sharp odour of palm oil. For the first time in two days on the road in Burundi, I ride past a factory.

I stop in Kiremba for food, parking at the only roundabout in town, where a man is grilling *chevre brochettes*: goat kebabs. Women join us wearing uncommonly elaborate hairstyles, set off by the now-familiar accessory of tinted sunglasses perched halfway down the nose. A crowd forms and there is a queue for lunch. A young English speaker who is home from college in Bujumbura helps out with translations. As I do my best with the meat, he tells me about life in the capital.

'I like Buja, the nightlife is wonderful. But it is so dangerous,' he says. 'If they think you have money, they will kill you. No rob, just kill. It is common. It happens a lot. It is better here in a small town for you as a *mzungu*.'

I am relaxing by the minute, and the crowd that has formed is slowly engulfing the bike.

'Take your bags off the bike,' the teenager tells me. 'Their hands will be in there.'

The cook, whose griddle is now packed with meat, charges me 500 francs, despite my agreement with her husband to pay 1,500 francs. I think she appreciated the crowd I attracted who stayed long enough to order food. As a tip, I throw her the last of four oranges I bought this morning, then I head south.

A curious feature of many homes in Burundi are the splashes of white paint thrown against the outer walls. Occasionally the entire house will be covered in random, graffiti-like scars that sometimes extend to nearby trees and fences. There is no obvious reason for it. At first it seemed that a number of houses were ready to be repainted (although no paint has touched these homes since they were thrown together), but now I see it is common. Perhaps it was not the owner of the house who splashed on the paint, but others wishing to identify them in some way. It remains a mystery to me to this day.

Mabanda, a sleepy place with an air of used-to-be about it, is the last stop before the Tanzania border. The road beyond the town is bashed up and sandy, and heads uphill. When I reach the top of the mountain I can see the communications tower that marks the frontier, three high peaks away, and begin to feel cast adrift. In fact the whole area beyond Mabanda seems cast adrift. Even though I am twenty-five rough kilometres from the border post, for all intents and purposes I am already in no man's land. Even in Burundian terms there is little or no development out here. I ride through a large, abandoned refugee transit camp that must be a leftover from the last civil war, and no doubt ready to be pressed into service, should the need recur. I pass little villages that probably grew to service the camp, but now find themselves down on their luck. The people, too, look in a bad way.

The only other traffic is either men carrying bananas on bicycles, or crowded taxis skidding to and from the border. Boys tending three long-horned cattle in a deep ford over the road refuse my passage until I pay a toll. Then previously idle men in a village jog alongside the bike while employing clever strategies for relieving me of more cash.

Lastly, and more memorable than everything I see this afternoon, I notice four blobs of colour on the horizon of the dirt road: a quartet of women, babies on backs, wear brilliant robes and swirl colourful golf umbrellas that create shadows like ghosts on the red earth.

14

LIVINGSTONE

The smartly dressed Tanzanian officials behind a desk in the immigration office give me a spirited arrival. They can see that I am glad to be over the border and to be speaking English once more.

'There is a tarred road!' says one, with mock amazement. 'It is so! And we drive on the left!'

It is both the most unnecessary and most welcome thing a border official has ever said to me.

On pristine tarmac I ride south towards Kigoma, a large town on the eastern shore of Lake Tanganyika. Something is missing. The shouts of '*Mzungu! Mzungu!*', and startled, dumbfounded looks on the faces of bystanders that say, 'Where the bloody hell have you come from?' and 'Will you take me with you?' I know for sure I am in a different country when I pass a bespectacled hitchhiker with a red electric guitar strapped over his shoulder. No case, just the guitar, like a lost Hank Marvin. Unfortunately he is going east, so I have to pass on by.

It is a relief to see restaurants open for business, people with purpose and a mellow atmosphere on the street. I know that everything from this point on will be measured against my time in Burundi.

I check into the High Tech Lodge.

'Why are you called "High Tech"?' I ask.

'Internet,' says the man on reception.

I check in and pay for the room.

'How do I access the internet?' I ask.

'The internet does not work.'

The sweetly polite guy also neglects to tell me that the noisy, room-sized generator I can see not far from my window and clattering like a toolkit in a blender, pumps away twenty-four hours a day. Maybe I'll get used to it.

After a warm shower I ride down the dirt track to the road, past the generator on its last legs – past a family eating al fresco next to the generator on its last legs – and spend the evening in what I can best describe as a scene from the biggest outdoor drinking free-for-all I've ever witnessed, in a beer garden that's laid waste with bottles and glasses and chicken bones. Everyone is sozzled. The waitresses serving bottles of beer solicit drinks for themselves, the men grilling chicken and frying cassava swig from bottles, and teens dancing in front of a screen showing music videos cruise the tables in the hope someone will buy them another beer. Every last one of them, pie-eyed.

A woman comes to my table with an unopened bottle of beer.

'May I open it?' she asks.

The man on the other side says to me, 'If you say yes, *mzungu*, you pay for it.'

The woman goes to the next table and asks once more, 'May I open it?'

A drunk woman who turns out to be a waitress sits down and places an unopened bottle of Serengeti on the table.

'Are you buying beer?' she asks.

'I have one.'

She looks at the man. 'He has one!' she says, disgusted, and walks off without the bottle.

Within an hour I have three unopened bottles of beer on my table waiting for me to give the command to flip the tops.

I eat a whole chicken, then ride back past the people sitting next to the generator who are now watching a television turned up to maximum. I make my way to my room through the completely dark and, apart from me, unoccupied hotel.

Next morning I don't want to get up. I'm so wiped out from the last ten days' riding without a break that I can hardly move. I stroll down to the group of people having breakfast beside the generator. The racket is extraordinary and gets into my bones. I feel my jaw tense and stomach tighten.

'Will you join us for food?' asks a middle-aged woman.

'They gave me an omelette at the hotel, thanks.'

'Please sit.'

I take a chair and can feel the earth shake beneath me.

'Doesn't the noise –' I begin.

'What is he saying?' asks an elderly woman.

I raise my voice.

'Doesn't the noise trouble you?'

Some blank looks. A teenager smiles.

'We lived here before the generator,' he says. 'Before the generator we had no electricity. Now we have electricity. Which is better?'

I ride ten kilometres south to Ujiji – even written in English the letters promise something exotic – the oldest town in western Tanzania, and once a slave trading centre from where Arabs and other traders exchanged slaves, ivory and various commodities gathered from the region. The region's slave trade was officially abolished in 1873, but continued here well into the twentieth century when the railway arrived in Kigoma a few kilometres to the west.

Ujiji means little to the outside world. But to anybody with half an interest in the European exploration of the continent, the town will always be known as the place where, after spending months hacking his way through the bush, Henry Morton Stanley met Dr David Livingstone and uttered the oft-repeated phrase: "Dr Livingstone, I presume?"

Locals know the cobbled-street district as 'Livingstone', which is now predominantly a sleepy Muslim neighbourhood. There is a hokey museum that tells visitors no more than they probably already know about the two explorers, considering they have made the trip in the first place, with a preposterous life-sized waxwork recreation of the meeting. The relatively expensive entrance fee and perfunctory guiding is a let-down, especially compared to the dramatic setting of the boulder memorial south of Bujumbura. Nevertheless, it does nothing to diminish my sense of arrival at one of the defining locations of Livingstone's extraordinary life.

Born and brought up in Blantyre, Scotland, Livingstone was a mill worker from the age of ten and dragged himself out of poverty to study at school, eventually graduating to college. Rather neatly he qualified as a medical doctor and was ordained as a missionary in the same month in 1840, thus simultaneously becoming a man of science and a man of God: two seemingly contradictory interests that defined his extraordinary character.

The following month he travelled to the largely undiscovered continent to convert the "Godless" tribes. Improbable as it may seem, over his entire missionary career in Africa, a span of thirty years, he succeeded in converting only one man – who returned to local customs very quickly. Later, the converted chief translated the Bible into his own language, so perhaps Livingstone was indirectly responsible for more conversions. If I were religious, at this juncture I would find a deft connection to the Parable of the Lost Lamb.

Livingstone's first mission station in present-day South Africa closed soon after his arrival because of drought, so he headed north into the unexplored interior. After three years travelling, he was attacked and badly injured by a lion. The poorly set broken arm and scars on his shoulder were apparent for the rest of his life. He then undertook a trailblazing transcontinental journey from Luanda in present-day Angola on the Atlantic coast, to Mozambique on the Indian Ocean. He became the first European to set eyes on the huge waterfall that locals called *Mosi-oa-Tunya* ("the smoke that thunders"), which he named Victoria Falls. Reports of his journey were greatly celebrated in Britain and cemented his reputation as an adventurer.

First and foremost a missionary, Livingstone nevertheless recognised the importance of trade in central Africa. His motto, inscribed now on the base of the statue dedicated to him at Victoria Falls, was "Christianity, Commerce and Civilisation". He hoped that this creed would form an alternative to "the open sore of the world": his description of the slave trade, which was still commonplace in the mid-nineteenth century. He believed that the "three Cs" would give Africans both dignity and bargaining power with European traders, who would no doubt follow in his footsteps. He also deduced the key to achieving these goals was the navigation of the Zambezi River, which might create a Christian commercial gateway into the interior.

1857 was a watershed year for Livingstone. He returned to Britain to raise money for a further expedition and to publish a book on his travels, which sealed his fame as one of the leading explorers of the age, and led to the Royal Geographical Society granting him its most distinguished award, the Gold Medal. The success of his book, *Missionary Travels and Researches in South Africa*, led to a growing belief that his spiritual calling was less about mission work and more about establishing new routes for commerce to displace the slave trade. He later resigned from the London Missionary Society after it demanded he do more evangelising, and less exploring.

Subsequently he was appointed by the British Government as Consul for the East Coast of Africa and given a grant to further explore the Zambezi. The troubled expedition lasted a staggering six years. He returned to Britain in 1864 after his funding was cancelled because of increasing costs and his failure to find a navigable route to the interior.

In 1866 Livingstone returned once more to the east coast of Africa, from where he set out to definitively confirm the source of the Nile: a discovery he believed would seal his reputation. Nine years after Speke had suggested Lake Victoria was the source (there remained much conjecture on that question), Livingstone was still convinced that the source was further south. With a team of freed slaves, Comoros Islanders, Sepoys (Indian soldiers) and two loyal servants, Chuma and Susi, he set out for Lake Tanganyika. However, the expedition went horribly wrong when his supplies were stolen and many members of his team abandoned him. The deserters explained their early return to the coast by saying that Livingstone had died and the mission was over.

Although the explorer completely lost contact with the outside world for five years, he believed that his sponsors and family back in Britain knew where he was, and had received all the latest news. However, only one of his forty-four letter dispatches made it to the mail ship in Zanzibar, which fuelled speculation about his fate.

In 1871, on the banks of the Lualaba River (in modern-day DR Congo), he witnessed the massacre of hundreds of

Africans by Arab slavers. The event appalled the ageing and ailing missionary, and persuaded him to give up his search.

In contrast to the large, well-stocked expeditions and often brutish methods that would later be employed by Stanley, Livingstone travelled light and applied an equally light touch in his dealings with chiefs across whose land he trespassed. Accompanied by a small team, and with the minimum of supplies, he was respected in many kingdoms, not least for his exceptional medical knowledge. He was the first medic to identify a link between the presence of mosquitoes and malaria. Before his discovery it was believed the condition resulted from bad air (*mal'aria*, as the Italians referred to it). He also noted the association between fever and tick bites, and correctly made connections between living conditions and diseases such as typhoid and dysentery. Consequently, his expeditions suffered less ill health than earlier European-led safaris.

Livingstone was wrong about the Nile, but that miscalculation does nothing to undermine his achievements as a great explorer who discovered many lakes, rivers and regions previously unknown to the Western world, and which perhaps can rank alongside the achievements of the Apollo astronauts who were more prepared for their destination. The few early explorers who had returned from Africa (many either died from infectious diseases or were killed) told lurid tales of slavery, cannibalism and deadly disease. What must it have taken for a young man from a small town south of Glasgow to step into an unmapped world, with the sole intention of sharing the word of God?

I recognise his fearless achievements, but I prefer to measure Livingstone against something he wrote in a letter to the editor of the *New York Herald*: "If my disclosures regarding the terrible Ujijian slavery should lead to the suppression of the East Coast slave trade, I shall regard that as a greater matter by far than the discovery of all the Nile sources together."

For a man who is still regarded as one of the greatest of his age, that is a modest and fitting tribute.

Stanley, who had been sent by the same newspaper to find the 'lost' Livingstone on an eight-month, 1,100-kilometre overland journey, found the explorer here on the shore of Lake Tanganyika in November 1871. Against Stanley's wishes Livingstone refused to return to Britain, even though he was very ill and his wife long dead.

Despite having six children back in the UK, he remained in Africa until his death on 1 May 1873. He died, kneeling in prayer, at Ilala (in present-day Zambia), suffering from malaria and internal bleeding caused by dysentery. His two servants, Susi and Chuma, who must surely have been his friends by now, removed his heart and buried it under a nearby *mvula* tree. They then covered the body in salt, wrapped it in the bark of a tree and attached it to a pole in preparation for perhaps the longest funeral march in history. They carried the body with his journal and instruments nearly 2,000 kilometres over nine months to Bagamoyo on the coast, from where it was shipped to England. His remains – still identifiable from his injuries suffered from the lion attack – were interred at Westminster Abbey.

In the footsteps of explorers comes Western civilisation, or at least a version of it. Seven years later the London Missionary Society established its first post on Lake Tanganyika and spread throughout central Africa, initiating church-led education and clinical health care, and continued the fight against the slave trade. Then came Western traders. Once Africa's potential wealth and strategic value was identified in Europe, the Scramble for Africa began in earnest and lasted until the outbreak of the First World War. Livingstone would not have recognised the kind of colonialism that followed.

I step over to two official monuments a couple of hundred metres from the receding water, but once on the lakeshore. The first is a simple plaque that reads, "On February 14th 1858, Burton and Speke reached Ujiji whence they explored Lake Tanganyika". It was from here, with Burton laid up with fever, that Speke continued north and discovered the vast stretch of water he would name Lake Victoria.

The other monument is an ugly, two-metre wall of stone with a relief outline of Africa. It reads: "Under the mango tree which then stood here Henry M Stanley met David Livingstone 10 November 1871".

Like Livingstone, Stanley became an explorer by circumstance. He was a journalist looking for a story and found himself in March 1871, with more than 200 porters, hacking his way from the coast through no-white-man's-land. By inserting himself into the celebrated explorer's story – his subsequent book was called *How I Found Livingstone* – Stanley established a tradition of first-person adventure journalism. The bestseller enhanced the reputations of both men.

Stanley made few friends on the expedition, and soon acquired a reputation for brutality with his porters. Among Africans he was known as *Bula Matari* – 'Breaker of Rocks'. Burton once commented, "Stanley shoots negroes as if they were monkeys."

Although the page in his diary that relates to his first meeting with Livingstone was ripped out, this is how Stanley subsequently chose to record it.

The head of the Expedition had halted, and the kirangozi [guide] was out of the ranks, holding his flag aloft, and Selim said to me, "I see the Doctor, sir. Oh, what an old man! He has got a white beard."

And I – what would I not have given for a bit of friendly wilderness, where, unseen, I might vent my joy in some mad freak, such as idiotically biting my hand; turning a somersault, or slashing at trees, in order to allay those exciting feelings that were well-nigh uncontrollable. My heart beats fast, but I must not let my face betray my emotions, lest it shall detract from the dignity of a white man appearing under such extraordinary circumstances.

So I did that which I thought was most dignified. I pushed back the crowds, and, passing from the rear, walked down a living avenue of people, until I came in front of the semicircle of Arabs, before which stood the "white man with the grey beard".

As I advanced slowly towards him I noticed he was pale, that he looked wearied and wan, that he had grey whiskers and moustache, that he wore a bluish cloth cap with a faded gold band on a red ground round it, and that he had on a red-sleeved waistcoat, and a pair of grey tweed trousers.

I would have run to him, only I was a coward in the presence of such a mob – would have embraced him, but that I did not know how he would receive me; so I did what moral cowardice and false pride suggested was the best thing – walked deliberately to him, took off my hat, and said: "Dr Livingstone, I presume?"

"Yes," said he, with a kind, cordial smile, lifting his cap slightly.

I replaced my hat on my head, and he replaced his cap, and we both grasped hands. I then said aloud: "I thank God, Doctor, I have been permitted to see you."

He answered, "I feel thankful that I am here to welcome you."

Stanley's trek was a staggering feat of endurance and perseverance. Three years later, the *Daily Telegraph* financed him to undertake an even bigger mission: to trace the course of the Congo River – an expedition that took 999 days.

After thirty-five days on the road, I cannot imagine continuing for another 964.

15

THE RED ROAD

That afternoon, in contrast to last night's debauched bar on the main street, I go to a frugally dry hotel that serves fish on clean plates and has a clientele that consists mostly of African non-governmental organisation (NGO) staff. Then I cruise the barbers along the main street. Who to choose: One Way Barbers, Shawn Shavers, Who is Perfect? I opt for SoSo Def Barber Shop. I am charged 5,000 shillings instead of the usual 3,000 because, I am told, 'Your hair is different.'

Next morning, I plan to ride the long road north-east towards Mwanza, to reconnect with the shoreline of Lake Victoria, a journey of about 700 kilometres according to the map. Everything about that sentence defines the optimism that sometimes overtakes me on these trips through Africa. The route is much tougher than I had anticipated – strictly speaking, tougher than I allowed myself to believe – and quickly turns into the dustiest, and reddest, stretch of road I have ever ridden. The narrow dirt road either has no edge to it or ends in a deep trench, so one false move could land me in a heap of trouble. There is no level section, and other vehicles fight me for the flattest part. It doesn't help that the morning sun is blinding and the fine airborne dust creates a permanent, shimmering haze. It's like Tanzania is shedding its skin.

After only 100 kilometres, the town of Kasulu is a welcome sight and I stop for a lungful of fresh air at an outdoor restaurant. After being joined at my table without invitation by a voluble character called Kahisha, I call it a day. What's the rush? Actually, I'm shattered, and I'm already coughing up gobs of dirty phlegm.

'It is my day off,' says my companion. 'I am warehouseman at the Nyarugusu Refugee Camp to the north.'

Kahisha drinks a Fanta and puts his feet up on the spare chair. He wears dusty black trousers and sandals, and his white shirt is more off his body than on it. His English is good: he gives himself the job of translating conversations at other tables for me, and my conversation for everybody else.

'Where have the refugees come from?' I ask.

'There are two camps: one for Congolese, one for Burundians. They have come from all over – 66,000 in number, most Congolese. They cannot work or move out of the camp; I think perhaps they will stay in our country. The government must make the decision to send them back, but I do not think they want to say yes. You have seen how Tanzania is: the road, the people, the way we live. Is there money here to care for refugees? To take them to our villages?'

'But the civil war in Burundi is over, isn't it,' I say, feeling my way.

'It matters not. The UN do everything they can to make them go home,' he says. 'But they tell me terrible stories. So terrible, I would not want to say.'

'But they have a home there, no?'

Kahisha takes this as the height of ignorance – which it is.

'If you were forced to watch your son rape your wife, could you go back to that village, knowing the people responsible are still there? Would you go back if your parents were chopped in front of you? Then you were made to eat their ears? Congo, too. Their arms are chopped, their legs are chopped. They tell me the only way they will leave the camp and go home is by gunpoint.'

His argument is so convincing it's depressing.

'I'm sorry for not understanding,' I say.

'It is not you, one man on a moto. What can you do? The *world* does not understand. Also, there are still refugees from Burundian wars from the 1970s. What is the date today? They have spent a lifetime here. What hope is there to go to their home village? The camp *is* their home. They are not Tanzanian, yet they are not Burundian anymore. Some, a few, are given the choice to become Tanzanian citizens. Most take it.'

'They don't have many choices,' I say.

'No choice,' he says. 'Choice is what you have on a moto with money in your pocket. But Tanzania does what it can. This poor country, this mix of one hundred and twenty languages united by Kiswahili, we help more than most.

Look where we are! Next to the DRC, next to Burundi, next to Rwanda – all countries with sorrowful histories.'

'I was in Burundi,' I say. 'Only two days, enough to know you have much more here in Tanzania. But I don't think there is any fighting there now.'

'The war is over,' he says, 'but some rebels are still in the bush, and Buja I hear is dangerous. Some Burundians will soon return to their country – the frontier is only forty kilometres across the bush. But most refugees are from Kivu Province in the DRC. You were there?'

'So close, I could almost smell it,' I joke.

'Close enough. Just across the lake, the fighting, can you imagine? The rebels come to Kivu, and the refugees come to us, and are still coming.'

'They're streaming across the border to Uganda too,' I say. 'I saw them near Goma.'

'Goma is too dangerous. The rebels go there too, follow them right into the camps and chop them.'

In a pause, I am handed an unidentifiable plate of food.

Kahisha spends the rest of our time together explaining my presence to people in a way that suggests I have come especially to see him. He has been stimulating company and I appreciate him taking the trouble to bring me up to speed on local events, but he's not finished with me yet. I ask the waitress if I can see a room above the restaurant to dump my kit and wash off the dirt from the Kigoma road, but Kahisha insists on taking me outside the town to a quiet hotel that has his seal of approval. It's perfect. We part with the shared knowledge that one of us is a little more informed about the refugee situation in East Africa.

Next morning the road onwards continues as bashed up as ever. In fact, worse. Even though the surface is quick for a dirt road, the bike is taking some terrible punishment.

I pass through overlooked communities filled with overlooked people. Homes are built from grass and straw with wavy roofs and indeterminate lifespans.

The dust hangs permanently in the air engulfing cyclists, passengers with their heads hanging out of bus windows (I can only imagine how bad it is inside), and burdened people walking. Anyone within twenty metres of the road is living in a fog.

Every bus and truck churns up the earth to fine dust, leaving people inches away moving like wraiths through a red cloud. Hourly I get a near miss from a bus or *matatu*. I yell warnings through the thick dust and hold my thumb on the horn, but no one would stop if they hit me; they would not even know.

The blinding light of the morning turns into a scorching afternoon, the uncanny heat turning the soil to ground red chalk and the bush to tinder. I am already daydreaming about all that water in Lake Victoria.

Next day, villages come, villages go, as I close on Kibondo. I see cotton stacked by the roadside waiting for pick-up, looked after by a bevy of shaven-headed girls dressed in yellow, eating raw sugar cane, hands on hips, like three posed figurines on a shelf. The image vanishes as quickly as it appears.

I am still on the Mwanza road, but now I'm moving through wide, open country. It is much hotter than Burundi and Rwanda – unsurprising, at the lower altitude – and the grassy plains dotted with low trees are better suited to cattle grazing. Little soil is under cultivation.

Up ahead I see a truck with Burundi plates lying on its side, with wheels akimbo. "Dieu Merci" reads the caption on the windscreen. Most of the lime the truck was carrying is now dumped on the verge and up a rough bank.

The man wielding a *knobkerrie*, who has been posted to stay with the vehicle to ward off scavengers, says the driver has been taken to hospital. He clambers up on the wrecked cab and does a little jig.

'Photo! Photo!' he calls.

I push on and find myself on a stretch of road that doesn't deserve the name. Maybe it's psychological, but the surface seems to be getting worse the closer I get to tarmac. Deep ruts, corrugations and unstable sand make for an unpredictable ride through thick bush. Homesteads are usually mud huts or mud-brick homes surrounded by nodding chickens and little allotments of corn burning in the fierce heat of the sun. Occasionally the road opens into great long straights with low hills and scrubby trees – classic, blazing hot savannah country dotted with long-horned cattle. I feel like boiled Irish.

I reach Kibondo, a town just big enough to warrant a couple of small hotels. I negotiate for a room with a guy who doesn't know his twelves from his twenties, so by the end of it I don't know what I'm expected to pay. I think it's twenty-something thousand shillings, which is not good value for a room directly over the courtyard where all of Kibondo life seems to congregate, and where the washing and cooking for the hotel takes place. Nor is it ideal when none of the curtainless windows will close, the lights on the balcony don't switch off and the bathroom consists of a bucket of cold water and an open drain.

By noon the following day I reach what I believe might be the end of the red road – a truck stop. I park and stagger up the incline to the little kitchen under a corrugated roof tended by a gaggle of women busy chopping, cooking, serving and washing. I take a seat. Everyone around me looks just as exhausted.

The women cook beef stew – essentially, boiled meat served in salty water with potatoes and chapatis. The meat, chopped directly on an old pine table, is thrown into large vats placed over open fires on the ground. The stew is spooned then potatoes are added to the plate by hand before it is brought to the table. There is a convivial atmosphere among truck drivers who are either taking their last breath of clean air before they tackle the dust storm, or those heading in the opposite direction congratulating themselves after finally reaching some tarmac.

Beyond Muribanzi, a one-horse town where I stop for bananas and water, I find the road that takes me to Geita, where I see a sign for a gold reef mine. Then, as if confirming the fact, I ride behind an open truck full of miners covered from head to foot in golden dust and debris who have just come off shift. Further on, at the first roundabout I've seen in a week, I see a handwritten sign that reads: "Let's preserve our culture by writing our own books using local resources." Amen to that.

Ten hours after I left Kibondo, and three days out of Kigoma, I reach the small ferry that takes me across the Mwanza Gulf – the very spot where Speke first set eyes on the lake – then ride on to Mwanza city.

At the gate to a comfortable lakeside lodge is a 6' 4" Maasai wearing a red robe and holding a baby in his arms. He says he is in charge of security and takes my bike from me. I think that's safe for the time being. Then – even though his striking form must grace many tourists' computer hard drives – he suggests *he* photographs *me*. I give him my camera and he clicks away. I realise why he is so keen to record the moment when I see the picture. I am completely covered in a thick layer of the red road from helmet to boots. After three days in the saddle I feel like Randolph Scott in *Ride the High Country.*

I order food from the sweetest, but most absent-minded, waitress I have ever encountered.

After waiting forty minutes, I ask, 'Is my pizza ready?'

'I don't think,' she says.

'I've been waiting ages. And I'm really hungry.'

'Oh! I did not know that you were hungry,' she says. 'Give me five minutes.'

I end the evening playing pool in the bar with the giant Maasai, while his wife looks on with the baby on her lap. Every time the boy cries the Maasai takes him from his mother's arms and cradles him in his red robes like a doll in a blanket.

Next morning I check the ferry from nearby Nansio to Ukerewe Island with an idea to eliminate some road miles, but decide that what I need is another day's rest off the bike and to take some time to appreciate the resort, which is beautifully situated on the beach. It is the weekend so, although most of the rooms are taken by white people, the beachfront is full of locals taking a dip and sipping sodas.

It's odd how Tanzanians are uniformly polite, greet me with '*Caribou*', initiate handshakes, ask from where I have travelled; but whites tend to ignore a lone white, sometimes pretending they have not seen me. Like the Yorkshireman I met on Bugala Island, perhaps they are disappointed Africa is not 'all black'.

I am tempted to stay a third night, but when I find my few items of laundry neatly placed at the foot of my bed I feel the pull of the road once more. I have travelled three-quarters of the way round Lake Victoria, and plan to return to the spot where I first saw the lake.

With my eyes set on a first stop in Musoma, just beyond the Serengeti Plain further around the lake shoreline, I get on the road. Road signs tell me the town is either 220 kilometres or 248 kilometres away. Whichever it is, it seems twice as long.

I am accompanied most of the way by low-flying hawks, which seem as common here as pigeons in London's Trafalgar Square. It is Sunday, and families are walking to church in clothes suitable for a disco in 1973. Shiny and satiny material, sequins and glittery tops rustle and glisten down the road. Perhaps they are all on their way home from an all-night party. Rice must be a staple food in these parts, as I frequently see the grains laid out to dry in perfect squares of white on tarpaulin or directly on the road surface. Also on the road is a remarkable number of dead animals, some freshly killed. No one seems compelled to move them to the side for dignity's sake. I have identified some as dogs but they could be the remains of any creature, ripped apart by the traffic and now providing an unexpected feast for vultures. Similarly, bicycle boda-boda riders looking for a fare gather under trees at strategic points along the route.

Riding into a fierce and unpredictable wind, I skirt the western edge of the Serengeti National Park, peppered with slow-moving giraffes and zebra grazing under acacia trees. I feel like a lost wildebeest that's escaped from the herd and drift off into the world of a natural history documentary, until I am cut up by a truck with the windscreen call sign, "If Not, Why Not".

Musoma appears to be having a siesta. It's closed. I find a hotel on the first floor of a modern block, which also runs an outdoor restaurant next door where the receptionist suggests I park the bike. It seems quite a vulnerable spot, but the space is deserted and the security guards will surely keep an eye on it. The other option – dragging the bike up two flights of stairs – doesn't appeal.

As I leave the restaurant, a man stacking chairs looks back at the bike and says, 'There will be music tonight.'

I take a nap, and am woken at eight o'clock by a boom-tastic bass groove echoing in waves down the street. I follow the sound to the open-air restaurant. Before I can check on the bike, the manager grabs me by the hand and says, 'Yes, yes, the bike is fine-fine.'

Wearing a white shirt with hanging cuffs and flying tails, baggy trousers and plastic sandals, he is clearly trying to create an ambience of dress-down chic.

He leads me to a counter, 'Here is your bar... beer?' Then he takes me into the busy kitchen, 'And here is your chef... which fish, please choose, we also have *choma*,' and then calls over a teenager, 'and here is your waitress. Perhaps chicken, and boiled Irish? Chips?'

He immediately steps to another table without waiting for an answer. I tell the waitress to bring me the largest fish they have and a beer to match.

'Cold or warm?'

'Cold beer; warm fish, please.'

I stroll around the grounds and when the manager returns, I happen to be standing under a wonky marquee in the centre of the dining area. Thinking I have made my decision on where I plan to eat, he picks up a white plastic table with three legs and drops it down in front of me.

'Hold it! Hold it!' he says, as I grab the table top.

He runs off, finds a fourth leg, and wedges it underneath. Then he drags a chair for me. This, of course, is being watched by everybody else in the place and I feel very self-conscious being the subject of the manager's attentions – and the only person sitting under a marquee, like some unsociable potentate. He leaves to fuss over someone else. He is into everything and reminds me of Songkok at the training centre in Iten: nothing is too much trouble – except when I ask for a fork. Eventually, he brings one with only two misshapen prongs that looks as if it's been used to clean out the plumbing. It's like eating with a fish hook.

Loud as the sound system is, the headline part of the evening hasn't really started yet. A young guy grabs a microphone and begins singing/rapping/yelling an accompaniment to the recorded music. It brings a crowd to the dance floor in front of two towers of speakers. Local fashion seems to consist largely of satin shirts and sunglasses, tight bell-bottoms and lashings of gaudy jewellery. From where I am seated I can see people jumping athletically high above the crowd, which elicits screams of delight from everyone.

I make my way to the edge of the dance floor, where two scantily dressed girls are gyrating and leaping around the two DJs. Then I look closer and see that my bike has been wheeled onto the stage. The dancers in turn pick their way up onto the seat of the bike and leap gracefully through the air. In-between times the DJs stretch out across the bike seat, like they're in a music video.

To no one in particular, I say, 'That's my bike!'

'Is it so?' says a woman next to me.

'My bike's on stage!'

I join two guys who are amiably drunk, which is pretty much par for the course as the drinks are the cheapest I have found on the whole journey. It seems everyone's intoxicated except me.

People take turns on the dance floor to mime along to local pop hits or dance crazy moves to pumping rhythms, each one ever more outlandish. The audience waves money at the dancers and tuck the cash into trouser tops or stuff it down blouses. When the performers are satisfied with their payment, and to the wild appreciation of the crowd, they hand the microphone to someone else.

The two barely dressed girls take to the floor once more and wiggle their behinds in some mesmerising moves to compete for tips. Their rear ends don't seem part of them, as their routines get ever-more suggestive. The older dancer guides one of the DJs to a chair in the middle of the stage and proceeds to stretch herself around him in every position from the *Kama Sutra* – and some new ones. He doesn't move a muscle (that we can see). Everybody is recording it on their cellphones and money is now flying onto the stage. She dances herself to exhaustion and drips sweat all over the DJ, bringing the crowd to a raging boil. It is a night on which reputations are made.

It is 1 a.m. and I am left alone at the table. It seems so long since I arrived that I order more food and a Coke. As I am waiting for the chicken and chips, an elderly woman takes advantage of the empty seats between us and sidles along to me. She indicates that she wants to dance by getting to her feet and clicking her fingers. She has no English, no sense of rhythm, and no teeth. I'm reluctant, to say the least. My food arrives and I offer her a piece of chicken hoping to distract her. She takes a chicken wing and puts it in her mouth, then with a greasy hand, pulls me to my feet. She's gripping my fingers like she'll never let go.

Now that she has moved into the light I can see that she is tiny and withered with wiry grey hair and bulging eyes. Maybe she is not as old as I first thought, but rather a middle-aged woman with some wasting disease. She looks decidedly unwell. But she's got a chicken-stuffed grin on her that seems fixed for the duration, so I have to see this through. The crowd on the dance floor has swollen with an odd mixture of people aged from sixteen to ninety-six, wearing both Western and traditional dress, glitter and jeans, make-up and T-shirts, high heels and flip-flops, manicured nails and dirty, bare feet. The music is freakishly loud and beer, gripped in unsteady fists, is being spilled on everyone as dead bottles are kicked around the floor. It is the dance floor of the apocalypse.

As chicken lady and I join the main group of effortlessly voluptuous dancers, my two companion drinkers joyfully nod at my dance partner with their fingers twirling around their ears – information that is both unnecessary and two minutes too late. With similarly uncoordinated limbs there's hardly room for us both to shuffle, let alone dance. She grips me ever more tightly as her shower of affection threatens to become Victoria Falls.

Then to my right someone falls to the floor: a man wearing a red T-shirt is splayed out on his back – but he has not fallen, he has been pushed. Not pushed, even – punched. As the crowd gives him some room, four men lay into him with kicks and blows. Blood trickles from his mouth and eye, and he has lost his shoes. In spite of the onslaught, the man manages to get to his feet by leaning on one or two people in the crowd who, as the music has not stopped, incredibly, are still dancing. A space is created and the hurt man stumbles towards my table. The four guys leap on him and he falls heavily in the centre of my chicken and chips. The table collapses and one of the pursuers picks up my bottle of Coke and crowns the man in the red T-shirt. There is now blood and food everywhere, but no space for us to get far enough away. There is a moment's pause when I realise I am hugging the old woman. Without thinking, I must have grabbed her by the shoulders in a protective move. The man is on the floor again and looks concussed, but his pursuers are not finished with him. In the best Western movie tradition, one picks up my chair and crashes it over his head, then again, and again. And again. No one will interfere. Finally the music and dancing stop. The woman is eager to see the extent of the man's injuries, but I pull her away. Insults and accusations fly around the space, but most are half-hearted, as nobody wants to get on the wrong side of these four guys. In the momentary pause, the injured man staggers to his feet with a look of the hunted and, with his head now as red as his T-shirt, runs to the exit. The armed guard at the gate takes a brief look at him but lets him disappear into the night.

The four men disappear too. I make my way to what's left of my table as the crowd returns to the dance floor. Within the space of two bars it is as if nothing happened.

The night is over for me. I take a last look at my bike, which has survived unscathed from the night's astonishing events, and prepare to return to the hotel. The manager, meanwhile, has missed all the excitement. He returns and asks me to describe to him what happened.

I try a lighthearted tack, and say, 'The man in the red shirt landed on my dinner! There was blood and chicken everywhere.'

'But you are fine?' he asks.

'Yes. But my dinner!'

'Sorry for that, but you still have to pay.'

16

THE LAKE IS CIRCLED

Early the following morning I cross the Mara River, then enter Kenya and make my way to Homa Bay, a town on the western shore of the lake. Farming seems less haphazard than in Tanzania, the road is smoother and has more road signs, and there's a little more energy about the place.

I need some home comforts, so I bargain hard for a hotel room with hot water and a mattress that I can easily sleep on. The receptionist asks me if I want Kenyan or tourist prices. I take my chances.

'Kenyan.'

'You are Kenyan?' asks the receptionist.

'Of course. Look at my bike. Local plates!'

I get Kenyan rates and am given a large, agreeable tent – European-on-safari style – into which I collapse.

Later, I am watching birds flit and soar when someone from the hotel comes up to see if I need anything.

'How close is the edge of the lake?' I ask.

'It is close, but you cannot see it because of the hyacinth.'

I look out to where he indicates. I can see a flat area of fresh growth for about one kilometre; beyond, the water.

'This is all foreign species,' he says, 'and it is strangling the lake. The boats cannot dock, so they cannot fish. It also brings some disease, they say, and takes the oxygen from the water. Maybe it will take over the lake one day and we will have no fish.' (There are *some* fish left in the lake; I eat one of them that evening.)

Earlier, I look for a bank to exchange the last of my sterling for Kenyan shillings. While I am waiting in the queue, a teller locks the outer door to new customers. After a forty-minute wait, the cashier tells me that he can only exchange currency for account holders. People behind me in the queue point to a customer service sign that reads "How're We Doing?" and encourage me to complain. I go to the manager's office.

'What's the point in offering foreign exchange if you don't serve foreigners?' I ask, a little more belligerently than I had intended.

She is politeness personified.

'Please take a seat. How may I help you?'

I explain the situation, the wait, the no-exchange policy, the fact that the bank is now closed and I have no local currency. She calls her head of operations and asks him, 'How can we solve this issue?'

The head of ops tells me, 'You were refused not because you are foreign, but because the banknote verification machine is not working. The teller did not want to say.'

'We must verify your bank notes before we accept them,' says the manager. 'Let me try another solution.'

She calls a rival bank in town, which is also now closed, and asks if they have a working machine and whether they would reopen for a 'valued overseas customer'.

To my astonishment, they agree. The head of operations walks me down the street, knocks loudly on the locked door of the bank and we are led in by two armed guards.

Every unexpected tale needs a punchline... the second bank offers a better exchange rate than the first.

Next day I ride north and get stuck in a traffic jam held up by a political rally in support of Prime Minister Raila Odinga. Protestors carry a casket with an effigy of the PM's one-time aide Miguna Miguna who, in a new book, has accused Odinga of involvement in the widespread tribal violence following the 2007 election. The protestors set fire to the casket and sing and dance around the flames. The police look on impassively.

I reach Kisumu and ride to the crest of the low hill where I first caught a glimpse of Lake Victoria six weeks ago, the official start of my own Empire Road. The journey around the lake is complete. I can't yet say if I am changed in any profound way, but I am left with an enormous admiration for the courage and character of David and Mary Livingstone, Stanley, Speke, Burton and other Europeans in the vanguard of exploration. The fact that there were few established routes of any significance never bothered Livingstone, of course, who was reported to have said, "If you have men who will only come if they know there is a good road, I don't want them. I want men who will come if there is no road at all."

I have also been impressed in different ways by the countries I have visited: Uganda's beautiful countryside and great curries; Rwanda's indefatigable spirit and optimism; Burundi's true grit in the face of crippling poverty; Tanzania's world-class ability to take it easy; and Kenya's diversity of people and landscapes that fuel the soul and makes travel in Africa its own purpose. Perhaps that is a hint of what Livingstone meant when he wrote:

> 'The mere animal pleasure of travelling in a wild unexplored country is very great... The effect of travel on a man whose heart is in the right place is that the mind is made more self-reliant: it becomes more confident of its own resources – there is greater presence of mind.'

Is this what I've come here to learn? To admire the feats of the great Victorian explorers, or perhaps to envy them?

I take a room at the irresistibly named Sooper Guest House, and go out to investigate the street life. I sit outside a cafe.

'Tea, please,' I say.

'Something to bite?' asks the waitress.

'Fish.'

'Pan-fried fish or deep-fried fish?'

Before I have a chance to choose, she adds, 'The chef prefers to deep fry.'

I spend the evening at the bar inside and by the time I am ready to leave, the street is deserted. I give the security guard, a long-limbed Maasai with a club and a weak torch, my doggy bag of leftovers and he walks me as far as the streetlight two blocks away.

Next day I leave the lake shore and ride the long, slow incline east to Kericho. The small farms make way for vast tea estates. Meanwhile, the warm sunshine is replaced with the wet and cold; by the time I arrive I am wearing every stitch of clothing I brought with me.

I check into the Tea Hotel, an imposing barn of a place which looks as if it might have been built soon after the Second World War, with all the fading colonial desperation that period implies. The hotel must have been a hoot in its day. The timing was ironic, because tea rationing didn't end in Britain until 1952.

It is clear that the hotel is begging for trade, so I bargain for Kenyan rates again and score a nice room with a view of the garden. I discover that the hotel was built by the British-owned Brooke Bond tea company – the people who made PG Tips. The tea company Brooke Bond was founded by Arthur Brooke when he opened a high-street shop in Manchester selling tea, coffee and sugar at about the time David Livingstone was 'lost' on the banks of Lake Tanganyika. The company, which changed its name to Brooke Bond because Brooke's 'bond' was his assurance of quality, still has a tea factory in Manchester.

The Tea Hotel's rooms are in small buildings scattered around the grounds in a recreation of an English village – or perhaps I've been roughing it for too long and it just seems that way.

The hotel does an admirable job of presenting a slice of British life, but unfortunately it's a vision that probably disappeared sometime in the late 1950s. I wish I'd seen it in its heyday. Inside, the lounges can't mask the institutional atmosphere; the staff, in faded formal wear, look institutionalised too. Stuffing seeps out of dated furniture, the once-beautiful parquet floors are worn and rotten in places, curtains, too short, hang askew on sagging hooks. Lights are mismatched and placed in unused corners and, as a reminder that I am in Africa, dusty, stuffed animal heads hang from walls.

The ambience of the hotel is not totally strange. Of all the countries I have visited, Kenya seems most determined to hold on to its colonial roots. Or perhaps there is just a vociferous minority that nurture familiar touchstones through simple things such as a reliance on tea, the use of tea cosies and cups with saucers, the driving on the left rule and familiar car registration plates: all things that remind the British traveller that they are not far from home after all.

I chat to a manager who shares my observations of the once-loved building. He complains of lack of investment following years of government involvement. It's another case of *If only*. The hotel and grounds (which seem to be subject to more care than the buildings) could be a big draw for the many tourists in the country, if they renovated the fixtures and fittings and charged double.

Save for a waiter in the corner, still as an old hat stand, I sit alone in the echoey dining room with a buffet large enough to feed fifty. The staff must be cooking for themselves. After a while, four people come in and pick at the food. I get into the colonial spirit and order a gin and tonic, after which the food makes an impression. The meal in the dining hall reminds me of a Scottish baronial pile I once visited, run by an oddball lord with just enough income to keep the electricity switched on and the phone connected. It needs an equally eccentric personality to save the Tea Hotel.

The rest of the evening is spent being mistaken for a member of the Kenyan legislature, when a seminar on crime prevention breaks up next door and takes over what until then had been my private lounge.

'I am very busy,' a magistrate tells me. 'There is a lot of crime!'

I like the hotel, even if the staff are fighting a losing battle with property maintenance. Nevertheless, the charm of the place seems to be relying too heavily on its attenuating ability to keep up appearances. The fun lies in spotting the gap between ambition and reality. 'We have internet!' means the receptionist has an occasional connection. 'Food is served on the terrace,' means I can take my cup of tea outside if I wish.

Like a nursing home, after nine o'clock there is nothing much to do except have an early night. The bed is made with cotton sheets tucked in so tight that if I got into it as it was presented to me, I might be there still. The night is cool and mosquito-free, and I dream of England.

I take the Nairobi road towards Naivasha. It hits me that this is my last full day on the road. Without thinking, I slow down and enjoy a heightened sense of appreciation of everything I have been taking for granted over the past few weeks. I spend a little extra time looking at a woman selling a mound of Irish potatoes, and a boda-boda wearing a headscarf inside his helmet; I notice the lie of a hill, the rows of corn in a field, the bare heels of a boy playing with a hoop and stick. I begin to miss them all.

I ride to Elsamere, the one-time home of Joy Adamson, the naturalist most famous for writing *Born Free*. It is a pleasant, colonial-style house that has been given over to the Elsa Conservation Trust, and is now surrounded by large, white-owned flower farms. I stroll around the grounds, which are overrun with shaggy black-and-white colobus monkeys, and enjoy the views out over Lake Naivasha. The 800 shilling admission fee includes afternoon tea, cake and pudding. I eat twice.

The house was named after the orphaned lion cub that Adamson raised called Elsa, with which she struck up a unique relationship. What is less well known is that her husband, George, shot the cub's mother, which was why it was an orphan.

It is my final day on the Empire Road. The tarmac is smooth with little traffic as I head south back to Nairobi. When the road surface feels a little uneven I slow down. But I soon realise that the front wheel is out of control because I have a puncture, the first in any solo trip I've taken through Africa. I pull into a lay-by where a stranded truck has its bonnet up, and two guys wait for assistance. After hailing a few cars and a postman on a moto for help – to no avail – the truck driver inspects the tyre and says he has a solution.

'You have a puncture,' he says.

'Looks that way.'

'So if I put some air, you can maybe ride further.'

'But we're miles from a pump.'

'My truck has air. In every tyre we have air. We must take the air from us and give to you.'

'The kiss of life!'

'Why not.'

I really didn't think it was any more than a fanciful suggestion, but he opens a container on the side of the truck and takes out an air line.

'I hold my side and you hold your side,' he says.

I fit the air line over the tyre valve, and on the count of three he forces the other end of the line over one of the truck tyre valves. Like an adder in the grass the line comes alive, and my flat tyre instantly inflates. In fact, it's probably ready to pop.

'The kiss of life!' he says. 'Go now. Go quickly before you are flat.'

I get on the bike and head down the road. Did that just happen?

The bike keeps going for seventeen kilometres – fuelled by the various prayers I am reciting – and just about limps into

Mai Mahiu. A man in a balaclava patches the punctured inner tube without removing the tyre from the wheel. He only asks for 300 shillings (about £2.25) for the repair, so I give him an unworn T-shirt as a tip.

Nairobi is exactly as I left it six weeks ago: the traffic hasn't moved an inch. I check into a guest house, then ride from boda-boda corner to boda-boda corner and ask at every workshop if anyone would like to buy the bike. Everybody looks interested; nobody makes me a cash offer. That evening I go to the pizza place where I had my first meal on arrival in Nairobi . The manager gets into conversation and I give him the highlights of the trip. He is especially agog at the events in the Kenyan desert.

'What now?' he asks. 'Do you ride home?'

'Back to Manchester? No, I need to sell the bike.'

'Do you need help? Shall I call Henry, the boda-boda?'

'You have Henry's number?'

'Of course.'

'Maybe he can help me find a buyer.'

'Maybe he will buy it!'

He makes the call.

'He will come,' he says.

And he does. I see and hear Henry before he sees me. He arrives in the courtyard on his battered bike, beaming at the Shineray.

'Henry!' I call.

'Present and correct,' he says.

'How does it look?' I ask, motioning to my bike.

'The sports bike has brought you back. I love this bike. I chose this bike.'

'You chose well.'

'How is the radio?'

He flips the switch, but the radio has died from all the downpours.

'No matter, I will fix. Now I should buy this bike,' he says, immediately getting down to business.

Like a good salesman, I point out how spotless the bike is (true), the fact that it has been serviced six times in six weeks (true), and how it has never let me down (a lie).

'The bike is perfect,' I say.

'I look after my bike also,' Henry says, looking over to his two-year-old, 37,000-kilometre wreck. The new helmet I gave him six weeks ago is unrecognisable, now with only half a visor and a ripped chin strap. It looks as though he's been playing basketball with it.

We haggle as Henry stares at the new object of his desire so hard, he's about to merge with it. We can't agree on a price. We continue haggling next day at the guest house. Henry is in danger of wearing out the words 'Please', 'Too much', and 'My friend'. Suzanne, the guest house owner, thinks Henry is taking advantage of me because my flight home is imminent.

'Do not trust these boda-bodas,' she says, making sure Henry can hear her.

Henry ignores Suzanne and keeps a fixed smile for me.

He says, 'I must try the bike for myself.'

'No problem,' I say.

'What?' Suzanne is aghast. 'Do not let him ride off with your bike!'

If Suzanne's eyebrows were any higher, they'd be lost under her wig.

'It's okay,' I say. 'He will leave his bike here.'

'Of course,' she says. 'Look at his bike!'

We all look over at the spent machine. Henry mumbles something to Suzanne that I take to be a quickly manufactured attempt at Nairobian flattery.

'It'll be fine,' I say. 'Henry, here's the key. Take it, but come back, hey?'

'You English!' Suzanne is disgusted with me and goes indoors.

Henry does return, eventually – probably via Mombasa. Now he is completely smitten with the green machine that made a failed attempt to cross the desert, met the elite athletes in Iten, was introduced to Mama Sarah Obama, rode up and down every one of Rwanda's thousand hills, starred in the 2012 Tanzanian floorshow, and finally rode around Lake Victoria. Which, now that I repeat it, sounds like something I should be proud of, but will soon just be part of the vapour trail of my life.

I tell him that he has until tonight to make a decent offer. Then I ask Suzanne to launder all my clothing. By the time that's done, Henry has returned with an improved offer and a pocketful of cash. Suzanne is astounded.

'My wife was telling me "Do not buy another bike",' says Henry. 'But I told her, "If you want to be successful in business, you have to take a risk."'

That evening I give away all the newly laundered clothing I'm not wearing and all my gear – every last item except my notebook, guidebook, camera and voice recorder. Boda-boda riders get the helmet, gloves, torch, bungee straps, wristwatch and waterproof gear; street people get toiletries and small notes and coins; the alleyway security guard outside the guest house gets my shoes and flashlight. It gives me a feeling of light-headedness, knowing that all the belongings I have left can fit into my tank bag.

Later, with 70,000 shillings burning a hole in my wallet, I go out to celebrate my return and my last night in Nairobi. I walk down Ngong Road intending to jump on a boda-boda, but a *matatu* pulls up and the driver asks me where I'm going. He has to turn down the blasting reggae on the cassette player before he can hear me.

'Not sure,' I say. 'Into town. Somewhere nice. I deserve a good meal.'

'To the New Stanley on Kenyatta?'

'Sounds good.'

'All the *mzungus* go there. We will guide you,' says the driver. 'Get in. Fifty bob.'

The driver pushes one of his front seat passengers into the back and tells me to replace him. The atmosphere on the bench-seat is like a stag party. The driver and the fare collector have both been drinking heavily, and the driver only keeps his eyes on the road for one second in every five. He shouts back to the packed *matatu* that he has now changed his route to suit me. To drown the jeers of disappointment he then turns Bob Marley back up to ten and heads off into the jammed traffic.

Acknowledgments

Quotation on page 97 taken from
Journal of the Discovery of the Source of the Nile
by John Henning Speke

Quotation on pages 191-2 taken from
*How I Found Livingstone; travels, adventures, and
discoveries in Central Africa, including an account of four
months' residence with Dr. Livingstone*
by Sir Henry M Stanley

Quotation on page 213 taken from
*The Last Journals of David Livingstone in Central Africa,
from 1865 to His Death: Continued by a Narrative of His
Last Moments and Sufferings, Obtained from His Faithful
Servants, Chuma and Susi, Volume 1*
by Dr David Livingstone, Ed. Horace Waller

We hope you have enjoyed this Inkstand Press book.
If you have, please tell your friends and
mention Empire Road on social media.

You can follow Alan Whelan here

Facebook: AlanWhelan10 / alan.whelan.writer

Twitter: @ACWhelan

Blog: www.abhaha.com

Web: www.alanwhelan.co.uk

Lightning Source UK Ltd.
Milton Keynes UK
UKOW03f0938281116
288702UK00005B/430/P